"Emily's invitation to embrace our weakness because God is strong will give you hope and encouragement for life's most challenging circumstances. Her personal stories and reflections along the way are a gift to any reader!"
—Ruth Chou Simons, *Wall Street Journal* bestselling author, artist, and founder of GraceLaced

"With refreshing honesty and biblical wisdom, *He Is Strong* turns our eyes away from ourselves and onto Jesus—the One who is able to give us strength when we are weary and courage when we are fearful."
—Melissa Kruger, author and director of women's initiatives for The Gospel Coalition

"The greatest desire of the human heart is to believe that even in our deepest inability—in our abject weakness—God still loves us and is in fact for us. Full of refreshing transparency and clear biblical application, these devotions will strengthen your soul and stir your affections for Jesus."
—Jared C. Wilson, pastor, professor, and author of *Love Me Anyway*

"*He Is Strong* offers time-tested wisdom to fortify the weary soul, wrap the reader with a comforting hug of encouragement, and lead us to the source of strength—Jesus Christ. This devotional will be a staple on my nightstand, serving as a constant reminder to accept my weakness as an opportunity to experience God's strength."
—Gretchen Saffles, best-selling author of *The Well-Watered Woman*, founder of Well-Watered Women

"To this day, whenever I feel overwhelmed with a sense of my weakness and inadequacy, that sweet chorus, 'I am weak, but He is strong,' infuses my heart with fortitude and grace. The truth of His unassailable strength and love will do the same for you."
—Nancy DeMoss Wolgemuth, author and founder of *Revive Our Hearts*

"Emily is the friend you want with you in the trenches. *He Is Strong* spoke to some of the most tender parts of my soul. Emily expertly weaves truth, light, and warmth through the entire devotional. You want to savor it, because it's such a comfort, yet at the same time you want to devour it, because it's so helpful. I recommend this book for everyone."

—Laura Wifler, author, podcaster, and cofounder of Risen Motherhood

"*He Is Strong* invited me to humbly consider my weaknesses while leaning into Christ's strength. With engaging stories and Scripture woven throughout, this devotional will encourage the fainthearted with the hope of their strong, steadfast God."

—Hunter Beless, founder of Journeywomen and author of *Read It, See It, Say It, Sing It!*

"We are small. We are finite. We are weak. When we admit our weakness, we can turn to God for his strength. That is the theme of this lovely series of reflections, which will bless all who are enduring a period of difficulty, a season of sorrow, or a time of trial. The Father's heart is inclined toward you and his hand is stretched out to bless and strengthen you."

—Tim Challies, author of *Seasons of Sorrow*

"With theological grounding and practical and poignant insights from her own life, she welcomes her reader to lean on Christ, who knows our weaknesses (and embraces them) better than we do ourselves."

—Amy Gannett, founder of Tiny Theologians and author of *Fix Your Eyes*

"Your weakness is a gift—an opportunity to lean on the strength of Christ and receive his help. This book will point you to the comfort of knowing that you do not walk alone."

—Russ Ramsey, pastor, author of *Rembrandt Is in the Wind*

HE IS
STRONG

EMILY A. JENSEN

HARVEST HOUSE PUBLISHERS
EUGENE, OREGON

Published in association with the literary agency of Wolgemuth & Associates

Cover design by Connie Gabbert Design + Illustration
Themed devotion artwork by Nathan Yoder
All other illustrations by Connie Gabbert Design + Illustration
Interior design by Aesthetic Soup

For bulk, special sales, or ministry purchases, please call 1-800-547-8979.
Email: Customerservice@hhpbooks.com

He Is Strong

ISBN 978-0-7369-8668-7 (hardcover)
ISBN 978-0-7369-8669-4 (eBook)

Library of Congress Control Number: 2023933496

Printed in China

23 24 25 26 27 28 29 30 31 / RDS / 10 9 8 7 6 5 4 3 2 1

*To all the
"little ones"*

CONTENTS

WE ARE WEAK

I reached down from my seat and felt for my water bottle until I heard it crunch between my fingertips. Silence hung in the air as I sipped. I tried not to make a sound, but the plastic bottle still crinkled loudly as I screwed the cap back on. Now that my throat was hydrated, it was time to talk. But what does one say in counseling?

Thought by thought, the words appeared. And over the months of meeting with my pastor, I found a lot of things to say. After witnessing a major medical event with one of our children, I needed to process it—to understand how my heart wades through trauma and to do it wisely, in light of the Word. Counseling has a way of walking through the connected paths in life, and eventually, we covered some important memories from childhood and a few thought patterns I picked up as a young adult. We discussed my inner dialogue in stressful situations and my default view of myself. I could have guessed that those aspects of who I am might make it into our conversations, but I wasn't expecting how many times I'd utter the word "weak." I sat tall in the armchair and carried on a calm, rational conversation, but inside, I quivered. I felt like a weakling.

Pictures popped through my mind like accusations—the time I quit acrobatics because I didn't have the mental toughness to do an aerial without putting my hand down at the last second, the times I gave in to peer pressure against my convictions of right and wrong because I wanted to belong, the way I transferred out of my far-off university in the middle of freshman year to finish college nearer the comforts of home. I've been a race quitter and an easy-way-out taker. I rarely snap my fingers and find the fortitude to make a desired change. I can't do anything I set my mind to. I don't like being told to tough it out. Trying to dig deep and fight harder only exhausts me—it doesn't motivate me. My mind replayed a montage of moments where I failed to stand firm or double down amidst failure.

Why is it that even under pressure and stress, when "life happens," some people seem immovable and press in while others quiver and buckle under the pressure? And why am I the quiver-and-buckle type, hitting my knees and asking for help to remove the weight?

Is my weakness a defect?
Is it something I need to change and overcome?
Why am I this way?
How can I find strength when I really need it?

The devotional you are holding is an outworking of my reflection on the different kinds of weaknesses I began to recognize in myself and a consideration of the hope offered to all of us in the midst of each one.

If you feel weak, if you think of yourself as low capacity, quick to quit, and easily overwhelmed, this devotional is for you. If you struggle with daily tasks because of chronic pain or you're worn thin by the burden of caregiving, this is for you. If you feel like the lowest and the last, perhaps overlooked, or you just don't feel as though you're very good at life, this is comfort for you. If you're beyond motivational speeches, tips, and tricks (though you've tried every one), this is God's word for you. In each devotional we will come to Scripture with our real questions and find hope in the midst of our weakness.

Maybe the idea of your own weakness feels unfamiliar and thinking about it doesn't leave you with tears welled up in your eyes or vigorously nodding your head. Instead, are you someone who tends to disdain your weakness—trying to avoid and fight against it at every cost? Or are you someone who wonders if weakness is a character defect and something to work your way out of? Are you someone who feels put off by the weakness of others and tends to think that most people are able to push harder, dig deeper, and work smarter to grow strong? If so, please don't put this devotional down quite yet. I've been there too, and I found that reading about the gospel and weakness helps us understand parts of ourselves and others—perhaps you'll find that instead of providing comfort, this devotional can soften you with mercy, compassion, and a true perspective of strength.

No matter who you are or where you're at, I pray the Lord uses these short reflections to point you to his help and strength as he has for me. But before you jump in, there are a few things you should know.

WHAT I MEAN WHEN I SAY "WEAK"

"Weakness" is a word with many meanings. It's used specifically and precisely, and it's also used as a blanket "feeling" word to cover many experiences in life.[1] Though each of us might describe weakness differently, in some way or another, it indicates a lack. Perhaps we call ourselves weak because we lack the muscle fibers and physical energy to lift a heavy box or move a dresser. For others, the experience of weakness reveals a lack of fortitude in the face of a struggle, the lack of power to resist temptation, or the lack of judgment when facing a difficult decision. We might feel we're weak because we lack the skills, abilities, motivation, and aptitude to do something. Weakness can express a lack of power or agency or potency. If weakness is simply something we don't have that we want or need for life—the instances of it are nearly endless.

As a concept, weakness can play a variety of roles. It's able to be used objectively, and relatively, and subjectively—even all three at the same time. Here's what I mean:

We can speak about weakness objectively. Often, defining something as "weak" is not influenced by our personal opinions or feelings, like when we say, "A newborn baby

---

1. The thoughts in this paragraph are based on the definition of "weak" in the Merriam-Webster online dictionary.

is weak." Anyone who has been around an infant for any period of time can see that they can barely hold their head up, let alone hold a heavy cup or lift a dumbbell. Though they are precious image-bearers whose lives matter eternally to God, they aren't yet mentally developed. They are weak in knowledge, discernment, and judgment. They are weak in agency and power, relying on their parents to survive. A baby is definitively weak—there's no need to argue about it. Weakness can be factually true.

On the other hand, weakness is relative. Saying "A newborn baby is weak" is still true, but context can change how I think about the concept of weakness. What type of baby are you talking about? A full-term newborn baby is strong in comparison to a preterm baby on oxygen in the NICU. The chameleon characteristics of "weakness" make talking about it tricky because there is almost always someone or something stronger and someone or something weaker depending on what perspective you're coming from.

Finally, weakness is subjective. For this example, let's think about a new mother. Some would say a new mother is weak because after just giving birth, her body is physically exhausted. She's likely losing a lot of blood and might struggle to walk easily depending on how her labor went. Because of hormones or complications or any number of factors, she might be emotional, sleepy, or even buzzing with words and energy. On the other hand, some would say a new mother is strong. Despite being exhausted, she wakes up multiple times over and over again to feed her new infant. If that baby is in the NICU or has complications, to the best of her ability, she fights for the health and well-being of that child. Her husband or her friends might look at her and see strength while she feels utterly weak and depleted.

As we explore weakness and the gospel in this devotional, which definition will we use? Will I be speaking of it objectively, relatively, or subjectively? All of the above. But to avoid as much confusion as possible, I use the phrase "feel weak" throughout this devotional. Because sometimes, though we feel weak, compared to someone else's experience or another person's perception of our actions, we're strong. As you work through this book, you'll notice that the title of each devotion helps you identify the type or feeling of weakness you'll be reading about.

THE STRENGTH YOU NEED ISN'T WHERE YOU THOUGHT IT WAS

Do you ever leave your house or apartment, walk to your car, and realize you misplaced your phone? Frustration sets in because you're running late and your phone is one thing you actually need. You check the cupholder and your purse. *Not there.* You run back inside to look in the last few places you were standing. *Not in the kitchen, not in the closet, not where I grabbed my keys.* And right when you lose hope of finding it and huff in despair, you reach around to your back pocket and realize it was with you the entire time. You just didn't stop to look in the most obvious place.

Our experience with weakness is a tiny bit like that. We

can often see that we're weak. That we're deficient in some way or missing something important—something we can't go without. We have circumstances we're facing that require our strength, ability, skills, knowledge, endurance, self-discipline, and resources. We have to find a solution because we can't go on. So we start grasping for what we need—we lift weights, buy habit trackers, follow inspirational influencers, research harder, ask friends for help, and store up money. And for many, when these things have only partial effectiveness or don't accomplish what we needed at all, we start to groan and despair. *What is wrong with me? Why is this so hard? What can I possibly do?*

Whether you're exhausted from studying for exams or under pressure as you set off to find your dream career, whether you're overwhelmed in the throes of the little years or feel defeated as you parent teenagers, whether you're trudging through another decade of unwanted circumstances or living under the debilitating effects of disease, whether you're weary from caring for a parent on the edge of heaven or starting to forget the most important details of your life, if you are in Christ, there is strength available for you. It just might not be where you thought.

Let's start looking.

HE IS STRONG

In 2012, my husband and I purchased a taupe rocking chair with square arms and white piping. When we assembled it in the nursery near the end of my first pregnancy, I imagined holding our future children, tired infants I'd sing to sleep in the dark. What I never imagined was rocking a son with disabilities, who'd spend more time in that chair with me than our other four children combined.

When he was an infant, I nursed him and cried because I couldn't understand why he struggled with feeding and growing. When he was a toddler (who wasn't talking or toddling), I rocked him to sleep after long days in doctors' offices, through tough questions and life-altering diagnoses. When he was a kindergartner, I still laid him across my chest, legs wrapped around my side, jammy feet hanging out over the chair arms—I comforted him through sick nights when he didn't have the words to tell me what was wrong. I haven't stopped rocking him yet.

In that chair, I prayed. I asked God some gut-wrenching questions. I sat in silence. But most of all, I sang. I don't have a beautiful voice and can barely capture a melody, but through many sorrows and late nights, I could sing. I'd gaze at the dim lights in the hallway or nuzzle into his ear or close my eyes, and then I'd rotate through every hymn I could sing from memory. "All Creatures of Our God and King." "How Firm a Foundation." "Come Thou Fount of Every Blessing." "Rock of Ages." "Amazing Grace." Eventually, I'd find the one I always finished with, the one I repeated until he was fast asleep: "Jesus Loves Me."

Sitting there in the quiet house, I'd play around with the wording. I'd sing it as "Jesus loves you," or I'd insert my name or his name. I'd sing it as a fact. As a cure. As a whisper in the dark. As my only hope. A streaming promise on loop.

One Sunday morning, in the midst of those early years, I turned the page of our sermon guide and saw that we were singing "Jesus Loves Me." I was unprepared for the effect it would have on me to hear a room full of adults join in the chorus of the rocking chair. It was so simple but so profound. So plain but so true. And perhaps my favorite revelation from that morning was the fact that the song includes more verses than the one I'd learned as a child. I came to treasure every word.

A SONG FOR THE WEAK

"Jesus Loves Me" originated in a story. In 1860, Anna

Bartlett Warner penned a poem for the second volume of her sister Susan's novel, *Say and Seal*. In the story, Mr. Linden sings "Jesus Loves Me" to comfort a dying child. Faith, another caregiver, looks on while Mr. Linden holds little Johnny in his arms. Here is the original scene:

> Faith had nothing to do but to look and listen; to listen to the soft measured steps through the room, to watch the soothing, resting effect of the motion on the sick child, as wrapped in Mr. Linden's arms he was carried to and fro. She could tell how it wrought from the quieter, unbent muscles—from the words which by degrees Johnny began to speak. But after a while, one of these words was, "Sing."—Mr. Linden did not stay his walk, but though his tone was almost as low as his footsteps, Faith heard every word.
>
> > Jesus loves me—this I know,
> > For the Bible tells me so:
> > Little ones to him belong—
> > They are weak, but he is strong.
> >
> > Jesus loves me—he who died
> > Heaven's gate to open wide;
> > He will wash away my sin,
> > Let his little child come in.
> >
> > Jesus loves me—loves me still,
> > Though I'm very weak and ill;
> > From his shining throne on high
> > Comes to watch me where I lie.

Jesus loves me,—he will stay
Close beside me all the way.
Then his little child will take
Up to heaven for his dear sake.

There were a few silent turns taken after that, and
then Mr. Linden came back to the rocking chair.[1]

There's my place of comfort. *A rocking chair.* The simplicity
of singing about the love of Jesus to a weak little one. The message a soul on the brink of death most needs to hear—one of
presence, comfort, and ultimate rest. A song for little Johnny,
for my son, and for everyone with the faith of a child who
aches for comfort in the midst of their weakness.

While the novel was largely forgotten, Anna's song was not.
In 1862, William Bradbury set it to a tune and published it in
a Sunday school hymnal.[2] Shortly after, in 1866, the song we
know today was also published in a larger hymnal with the
refrain "Yes, Jesus Loves Me," plus small alterations to help the
song make sense out of the context of the original story. "Jesus
Loves Me" went on to become one of the most well-known
hymns in modern history.

A SONG OF HOPE

Though most people can sing the first verse, it's time we
learned the rest by heart, because from beginning to end,

1. Anna Bartlett Warner and Susan Warner, *Say and Seal*, vol. 2 (Philadelphia: J.B. Lip-
pincott and Co., 1860), 115-16.

2. The Bradbury hymn is more similar to what we sing today: Anna Bartlett Warner,
"Jesus Loves Me," Hymnary, 1862, https://hymnary.org/ hymn/BGSS1862/68.

it shares Jesus's steadfast love and strength in the bleakest circumstances.

JESUS LOVES

> Jesus loves me—this I know,
> For the Bible tells me so:
> Little ones to him belong—
> They are weak, but he is strong.

For reference, see
Psalm 19:7; John 3:16,
15:9, 13; 2 Timothy 3:16;
1 John 3:16, 4:19

The first stanza of "Jesus Loves Me" is personal. The song doesn't just reflect on Jesus's love for mankind or his church in general but on Jesus's love for "me" specifically. For whoever opens their mouth to sing. For those who struggle to confidently speak a proclamation of Jesus's love out loud, the second line rushes in like a confident child's retort: "For the Bible tells me so!" In case there was any doubt of Jesus's love, the authority of Scripture shores it up.

On the firm foundation of Jesus's love, proven by God's Word, an identification statement is made. Who belongs to Jesus? Little ones. "Little ones" can be taken literally to mean a child (especially considering the context of the original poem), but figuratively, the term represents the children of God. The sheep that the tender shepherd, Jesus, carries in his arms. As we see ourselves as little ones, we're included as those who belong. Just as we observe the contrast between father and child, shepherd and sheep, the song declares who is weak and who is strong. Strength doesn't belong to the little ones but to Jesus Christ, the Lord.

JESUS SAVES

Jesus loves me—he who died	See John 14:3-6;
Heaven's gate to open wide;	Romans 5:8;
He will wash away my sin,	Colossians 1:21-22;
Let his little child come in.	1 Timothy 2:5; 1 Peter 2:24

While it's comforting to know that Jesus loves us, thinking and singing about warm fuzzy feelings isn't enough. Those who are little and weak need more than words—they need protection from death. Anyone who has taken a young child to the ocean or the zoo or who has simply stood beside the road or a cliff knows that. The second stanza addresses the way Christ loves us, by taking action to meet our deepest need and provide ultimate protection—washing away our sin so that we can be with God in heaven forever.

In the Gospel of John, Jesus makes a powerful and unexpected statement about his love: "Greater love has no one than this, that someone lay down his life for his friends" (John 15:13). Jesus showed this great and perfect love for us when he died the death we deserved and bore God's wrath so that we could live in righteousness. When we are washed clean by the blood of Christ, we aren't just loved, we are welcomed in—into the family of God, into union with Christ, into friendship with God, into a life filled by the Spirit, and ultimately, into heaven to live with God eternally.

JESUS SEES

> Jesus loves me—loves me still,
> Though I'm very weak and ill;
> From his shining throne on high
> Comes to watch me where I lie.

See Psalm 16:11, 139:7;
Matthew 11:28-30;
Mark 2:17

At this point in the song, all of our ultimate fears and concerns have been addressed—we're loved and saved by Jesus. *Eventually, all will be okay! We'll be with him forever!* But what about life today? If the previous stanza had us dwelling on our certain future hope, this one rips us back to our present reality. Though a glorious eternity awaits, today we still struggle. We still need Jesus's love in the midst of our grief, pain, and weary striving. The third stanza gives us a picture of a captive refusing to give up hope, though their captor tells them no one is coming to the rescue. *Yes . . . yes, he is. Jesus loves me, loves me still!*

Whether through physical weakness and illness or in the many other ways we experience weakness on this side of heaven, this stanza gives Philippians 2 imagery, reminding us that Jesus already left his throne on high to take on flesh and dwell among us, that he's alive, and that he's coming back again. Jesus has never been too lofty to see our pain and come to our side—he's gentle and lowly of heart, moved to compassion, present, and near to those who are weak.

JESUS STAYS

Jesus loves me—he will stay	See John 10:28, 11:25-26;
Close beside me all the way.	Romans 6:23;
Then his little child will take	Philippians 3:20-21;
Up to heaven for his dear sake.	Revelation 21:3

This last stanza comforts the anxious, fearful child in all of us. Jesus will not abandon us when things get hard—we don't need to panic (though we can certainly cling). He will stay beside us all the way.

All the way to where? you might ask. All the way to the grave. And while that may seem like a bleak way to end a song, isn't it deeply comforting? To know that the scariest place we can imagine going will not be a place without Jesus's loving presence? Even if and when we breathe our last breath—whether in childhood or old age—he will never leave or forsake us. He will stay until we exhale and be our sight on the other side.

HE IS STRONG

A theme weaves like a thread through this hymn: that we are weak, but Jesus is strong. While he experienced many of the "weaknesses" that we do—like when we're tired or hungry or grieving—he himself is not weak. In the beginning he was with God and he was God—all things were made by him (John 1:1, 3). Hebrews tells us that Jesus is "the radiance of the glory of God and the exact imprint of his nature" (Hebrews 1:3). He willingly left his throne to take on flesh, he obeyed God to the point of death—never giving in to temptation—and after he made atonement for sin, he went back to his throne, seated at the right hand of the Majesty on High (Philippians 2:6-8; Hebrews 1:3). "In him was life" (John 1:4). In every way, as a creator, prophet, priest, king, shepherd, bridegroom, messiah, and lamb, he exudes strength, goodness, and perfection. Jesus, just like every member of the Trinity, is fully God—all-knowing, all-present, and all-powerful. He has ownership of, access to, and ability to use every resource. He is never deficient, he's all-sufficient. And he loves us. He wants to help his children. This is why we look to the Lord for strength.

Throughout this devotional, I'll weave with the same thread from the hymn "Jesus Loves Me"—our weakness, God's strength—and reflect on common experiences of weakness through the lens of the gospel. Each devotion begins with a single verse from Scripture and additional readings from the Bible. Reading the verse at the beginning of each devotion in the context will ground you in God's Word straight from the start. As you answer the reflection questions and consider what God's strength means for your life, you'll need to be guided by the Spirit in prayer and truth.

As you reflect on each Scripture, topic, and question, you'll realize that I don't give you all the answers, but I aim to point you to the One who knows all things. The strength, hope, and help you're looking for are found in God, whose promises will cradle your heart with comfort and rest as you walk through life. Yes, you are weak, but you are not alone, lost, unseen, unprotected, or forgotten. At every stage of life, you're weak, but he is strong.

DEVOTIONS

1

WHEN YOU'RE AT THE END OF YOURSELF

Woe is me! For I am lost; for I am a man of unclean lips, and I dwell in the midst of a people of unclean lips; for my eyes have seen the King, the LORD of hosts!

ISAIAH 6:5

My hands gripped the steering wheel like I was driving through a thunderstorm, but the car wasn't moving. I sat in a dark parking lot with my hands at ten and two while tears streamed down my cheeks. Not the pretty kind you might see in an old film, where a single tear can be gently dabbed away with a tissue. My chest heaved, and I wailed more like a child than the twenty-year-old woman I was. It was a cry from the deep—not just tears for another failed relationship but the physical response of disappointment heaped upon disappoint-ment, mess upon mess that I'd made of my life. I'd lived apart from God, but *could I even call it life?* For all I'd done and tried, I had nothing but ruins to show for it.

I was desperate and confused. My thoughts weren't linear, and for once I had no optimism or clever plan. I sat in my car with no strength left and nothing to offer. My inner defense lawyer had given up my case, slammed down her papers, and walked out of the courtroom. I was open to judgment. For the first time in my adult life, I raised a sincere cry to God. With head low, I could mutter only two words: "Help me."

And help he did.

Within the week, I heard the gospel and believed. I surrendered my life to Christ. God helped me not by instantly cleaning up the mess I'd made of life but by giving me new life in him.

When I look back on those moments, nearly twenty years ago now, I think of the deepest kind of weakness a person can experience. Something worse than being keeled over with back pain or feeling insufficient for a task. It's the kind of weakness that each person must reckon with before a holy God. Our souls suppress it because we don't want to face how minuscule, broken, dead, and incapable we are apart from him.

Knowing you need a strength outside of your own might be something you considered at such a young age that your memory of surrendering to Christ comes in shadows and flashes. You've spent your life walking with God and experiencing joy in Christ, even though it's not been a perfect journey. Through the doubts, the ups and downs, you know the weakness of your flesh and your need for grace. For as long as you remember, you've lived as a debtor forgiven and saved.

Or perhaps, as in my case, God opened your eyes and ears to the gospel as a teenager or young adult, and you made the walk of a prodigal into the arms of your heavenly Father. He gently sifted your life through a colander, his loving hands shaking away every worthless thing, leaving only bits to build from as you walked forward in faith and obedience.

Or maybe you've never reckoned with your weakness. Perhaps you're tired, overwhelmed, discouraged, worn down, and frustrated with your own striving. You've tried every option for hope and help under the sun, and you're out of ideas. You sense a weight on your soul heavier than you can lift, and it's pressing your knees to the ground. Oh, friend, low is exactly the right direction to go.

In the book bearing his name, Isaiah, an Old Testament prophet, describes his vision of God. Seeing the Lord seated on a throne, surrounded by fearsome heavenly beings and quaking foundations, Isaiah cried out, "Woe is me!" In modern English, we don't use the word "woe" to describe our feelings. But Isaiah's vocabulary included "woe," and he would have used it to reflect deep despair and desperation. His listeners would have known "woe" was a cry full of passion and lament—almost an involuntary reflex. For Isaiah, "woe" was a sinner's wail upon seeing a holy God. And he brings us further into his state of mind when he adds, "I am lost. I am a man of unclean lips." I love the King James Version's translation: "I am undone." When Isaiah finds himself face-to-face with perfection and holiness and unimaginable glory and power, he instantly recognizes his weakness, confesses his humble state, and laments over his sin.

At some point or another, like Isaiah, each of us will be undone. You'll kneel before the one true God (Isaiah 45:23; Philippians 2:10-11). You'll cry out and feel exposed in your sin (Revelation 20:11-15). This can happen now, or it will happen later, at the second coming of Christ and final judgment. The certainty of our humbling is why Scripture implores us, "*Today*, if you hear his voice, do not harden your hearts" (Hebrews 3:15, emphasis added). The gospel, or the good news, is that each of us can turn to him for grace now, while the joy and reward are immediate, abundant, and eternal. God promises to do for us what he did for Isaiah, taking away our guilt and sending us on mission (Isaiah 6:6-9).

As we move forward in this devotional and consider many types and experiences of weakness, it's important to have this facet of weakness settled. Our soul-level weakness is not just a feeling and it's not imagined—the Bible says that all have sinned and fall short of the glory of God (Romans 3:23). But it also says that the grace of God appeared in Christ to save sinners like me and you (Titus 2:11). The strength of our holy God is exercised on behalf of our weakness.

Today, if you feel weak because you've made mess upon mess of your life, or because mess upon mess has been heaped upon you, let the weight drop you low. Collapse beneath the load in sweet relief. And leave the weight of your weakness again at the feet of Jesus Christ. There is no reason for you to try to clean up the mess in a strength you don't possess. Instead, cry out to Jesus Christ. He allowed himself to be crushed so you could walk freely today. And he lends his ear to every "woe."

⫸ *Additional Reading* ⫷

> Matthew 11:28-30
>
> Philippians 2:1-11
>
> Isaiah 6

⫸ *Questions for Reflection* ⫷

I am weak

- Have you ever considered who you are in relation to a holy God? Spend a few minutes reading and reflecting on the passage in Isaiah and consider what it means for your life.

- What aspects of life have left you feeling undone? Share them with the Lord.

He is strong

- What is God's response to those who come to him undone, needing salvation and hope?

- How does it change your perspective on your life and weakness to be free of the guilt of sin and find new life in Christ?

2

WHEN YOU SEE YOUR WEAKNESS EVERYWHERE

Let us run with endurance the race that
is set before us, looking to Jesus.

HEBREWS 12:1-2

On vacation in Florida, my oldest son asked me to name my dream car. Weaving between palm trees with light flickering through the open sunroof, I turned to my captive back seat audience and said, "If I lived down here? A white Jeep Wrangler Rubicon."

"But, Mom, what does that look like?"

From that point on, we were on a mission to spot a Rubicon in the wild. And once we saw one, they started to pop up everywhere. I spotted them in the neighborhood where we were staying. They were parked near the beach and driving down the highway. I'd never noticed before, but white Jeep Wrangler Rubicons are popular in South Florida. Even after we settled back into Iowa life, I kept seeing them everywhere. There's even a Jeep owner that drives my "dream car" down our street several days a week.

Have you ever had this phenomenon happen to you? Someone points something out and then you start to see it everywhere? There's a name for that experience; it's called "frequency illusion," otherwise known as the Baader–Meinhof phenomenon.[1] It has everything to do with selective attention because we pay attention to the things we're already looking for. It's a form of confirmation bias.

Frequency illusion isn't a big deal when it comes to noticing Jeep Rubicons in small-town Iowa, but what about when it comes to spotting our flaws? For those of us who've seen our weaknesses, it's possible to focus selective attention on our inabilities. People need to see their weakness, letting it humble them in dependence on the Lord, realizing they have no reason to boast. But for some of us, seeing our needs escalates to staring at our weaknesses all too closely, as if mulling them over will help us overcome them. Some of us let the reality of our weakness become a fixation and fixture of our identity.

When we give selective—even obsessive—attention to our weakness, we don't just see our flaws and insufficiency; we let the pain of it settle into our bones. We start to look for our

1. Wikipedia, s.v. "Frequency illusion," https://en.wikipedia.org/wiki /Frequency_illusion.

weakness, and we see it everywhere, prompting the narrative, *I'm so pitiful and pathetic. I'm so bad at everything. Why am I so useless?* When our weakness is the focal point of our story, we begin to pull back from kingdom life convinced we don't have what it takes to live a life of faith. If we become what we behold, and we constantly behold our weakness, we'll eventually give way to despair.[2]

I'm so bad at being creative and fun with kids; I'd be a useless Sunday school teacher.

I'm so awkward; I might as well just stay home instead of meet up with friends.

I have such a low tolerance for discomfort; I ought to say no to that mission trip.

I'm already the least popular mom on the PTO; if I talk about my faith, it will just make it worse.

Looking at our inabilities and weaknesses does nothing to equip or condition us to run the marathon of faith throughout our life. Yes, we have many weaknesses, but we are running a path blazed by Jesus Christ himself, and he has called us to follow in his footsteps, has filled us with the power of the Spirit to keep placing one foot in front of the other. We might seem insignificant, but we're a chosen part of an epic story serving a perfect hero.

That fixation reflex is right, but not on ourselves. Instead we need to fixate on Jesus, the founder and perfecter of our faith, not our flaws (Hebrews 12:2). Where we see "weakness,

2. Sometimes introspection can lead to depression. If you have deep, persistent, and ongoing feelings of despair and rumination, please reach out to a pastor, doctor, or licensed professional for help.

weakness, weakness," we need to practice seeing "Jesus, Jesus, Jesus." Instead of obsessing over the myriad ways we're unqualified, unable, and insufficient, we need to rehearse how he is qualified, able, and fully sufficient. Time is too short to tell every story in the Scriptures that proves Christ's sufficiency, but the multitude of other believers, running with Christ's strength in the midst of their own weakness, also shows us this is true. The endurance and capability of Jesus have been conveyed to us by the cross, and he is our all in all.

Are you wasting away while you count your weaknesses? Are your spiritual muscles atrophying? You don't have to deny your weakness to lay aside its weight and look to Christ. The author of Hebrews argues that we need to stop navel-gazing; we need to recognize the power of Christ in us, throw off our sin, and get rid of anything that's holding us back from running the race of life. If we don't want to grow weary of doing good, we'll "consider" Christ (Hebrews 12:3).

When we consider Christ, we can say yes to volunteer opportunities at church we know we have the capacity for, even though we're not 100 percent qualified in that area yet. We can be self-forgetful when we're out with others, focusing on how we can love and serve them in conversation. We can go on the mission trip, giving our fears and discomfort to the Lord. We can boldly talk about our faith, knowing our greater mission and security is in Christ. This is not because we've suddenly become strong, but because we have faith that the Spirit will propel us forward in spite of our many weaknesses.

⟫ Additional Reading ⟪

> Hebrews 11:1–12:3
>
> 2 Corinthians 12:5-10
>
> Romans 8:25-27

⟫ Questions for Reflection ⟪

I am weak

- Do you struggle with "frequency illusion" when it comes to spotting your weaknesses? How do you know?

- In what ways is it helpful to see and acknowledge your weakness? In what instance has focusing on your weakness hindered your kingdom work?

He is strong

- Based on the Scriptures above and your own personal experience, what evidence do you have that God isn't hindered by your weaknesses and will help you in the midst of them?

- What would it look like to "consider Christ" in your life today? How could you practice seeing Jesus's strength, grace, and power everywhere?

3

WHEN YOU DON'T HAVE ALL THE ANSWERS

*Now when they saw the boldness of Peter and
John, and perceived that they were uneducated,
common men, they were astonished. And they
recognized that they had been with Jesus.*

ACTS 4:13

In the fall of 2009, I pulled into an unfamiliar church parking lot to attend an unfamiliar thing called a Bible study. As
a newlywed and a new believer, I was looking for ways to meet
other women in our area and grow in my walk with the Lord.
Since my husband and I hadn't settled on a church quite yet, I

took a recommendation from a friend and decided to try Bible Study Fellowship.[1]

It was humid and I was already running a couple of minutes late. I hunted for a parking spot and hurried in alongside moms lugging toddlers as women in tailored tweed jackets and stylish flats swung the church doors open to greet me. Within a few heartbeats, I could tell this was more than I bargained for. I almost walked out but was so mesmerized by the wealthy suburban women singing hymns that I collected my name tag and found a seat in the back.

For thirty weeks, I walked through those church doors to study the Gospel of John. Each week, I'd struggle to complete my homework, and I'd skip over what I would now consider to be the most basic questions. I sang in a whisper during worship because I didn't know the melody of these apparently "classic" hymns. Praying out loud made me sweat and mumble pat phrases over and over. Though I'd carried my Bible everywhere for the better part of three years and I'd read it frequently, formal Bible study showed me I didn't know what much of it meant. I was held by the gospel of grace as I grasped for understanding.

Maybe you're a new believer and you can relate to being in over your head with Bible study. You show up to church and are moved by the sermon, but there are a lot of things you still don't understand. You smile and nod in deep conversations

---

1. Bible Study Fellowship is a global, nondenominational Bible study that I participated in in two cities over the course of about seven years. Visit https://www.bsfinternational.org/ for more details or to find a study in your own area.

with older believers, but later, you Google words like "justification" and "orthodoxy" to find out what they mean. You know the feeling of being weak in your knowledge of God, and you hope you can catch up before somebody catches on.

Or maybe you've been in church all your life and you think you have no excuse for not knowing the answers. You've attended decades of Bible studies and listened to countless sermons, but sometimes you still question elementary doctrines and forget the finer details of your faith. As a seasoned believer, you don't want to come up short with your Bible facts and look foolish.

There's good news for those of us who are still learning—no matter what leg of the journey we're on. Though God wants us to grow in our knowledge of and love for him (Philippians 1:9-11; 2 Peter 3:18), he doesn't need us to look super smart and impress people with all the big words we know. Though some Christians will be brilliant, glorifying God through intelligence, research, and clear communication of truth, those qualities aren't the only way to give God glory. Ultimately, Christians aren't recognized by *what* we know but *who* we know.

This was the case for two of Jesus's apostles in the early church—Peter and John (Acts 4:1-22). They stood on trial before some very important religious leaders who demanded answers and explanations. *How and why had they healed a lame man? Why were they preaching about the resurrection?* When Peter responded to the council, he spoke through the power of the Holy Spirit (Acts 4:8). The answer to the religious leaders' questions boiled down to a name they didn't want to hear: Jesus Christ.

Peter and John were not the kind of men with verified blue check marks on their public profiles. They weren't Ivy League grads or on track to launch the next big tech startup. They weren't about to whip out a bunch of research studies on healing and quote famous philosophers on the resurrection. They were just common men—average guys you'd walk by and not even notice. But their ordinariness was the perfect contrast to the brilliance of Christ.

As you go about life today and fumble to find a helpful piece of advice for a hurting friend or a clear and convincing response to your child's toughest spiritual question or the right answer to this week's Bible study question, don't despair. If you know Christ, you already know the most important person and the most important truth (John 17:3). In spite of all you don't know, it could be your humble boldness and simple explanation of Jesus that cause your friend or your child or your fellow churchgoers to marvel and grow. Not because of you but because of him. And isn't that what you want after all?

Additional Reading

Acts 4:1-22

Jeremiah 9:23-24

John 17:3.

⋙ *Questions for Reflection* ⋘

I am weak

- Where are you on your journey of knowing God and understanding his Word? In what areas do you still fear looking weak and foolish, even if you've been a believer for a long time?

- Why is it so scary to not have all the answers? What do you hope to gain by having more Bible knowledge or theological prowess?

He is strong

- How might believing the gospel, knowing Christ, and being filled with the Spirit equip you to glorify God in a regular situation today?

- How does knowing that God is able to work mightily in and through anyone (even "uneducated, common men") give you hope and courage? What action steps might you take to share more boldly or keep learning?

4

WHEN YOU FEEL INSIGNIFICANT

*Now there are also many other things that Jesus
did. Were every one of them to be written, I
suppose that the world itself could not contain
the books that would be written.*

JOHN 21:25

I used to be a competitive dancer. Most weekday evenings and Saturday mornings throughout my childhood, my parents drove the twelve minutes to my dance studio where dedicated teachers honed my technique and drilled our routines. But no matter how many hours I spent on pirouettes and jetés, in a group of elite dancers I was just . . . average. I was familiar with standing in the middle or back row in a formation—maybe making a short appearance in the front corner every now and then.

One summer evening at the studio, when the sweat was beading down my leotard and we'd done the same "five, six, seven, eight" a maddening number of times, the moment came for the teacher to assign solos. I held my breath. My heart palpitated because I desperately wanted to hear her call my name. But she never did. Holding back hot, angry tears after a long night of practice and years of being "overlooked," I murmured my disappointment to a nearby friend. "Why do the solos *always* go to the same people?"

"Emily, what did you just say?" The teacher's voice cut through the group. My stomach dropped, and the talking ceased. Immediately regretting my comment, I had no choice but to repeat the question in front of the whole group.

The teacher's words are lost in my memory, but her pursed lips, her furrowed brow, and the longing behind my question are not. While I chose a rude and childish way to express my disappointment, my concern about being part of the selected few outgrew childhood. It followed me throughout life, and maybe it follows you too.

Maybe you long to hear your name called for a special honor or recognition, but it never is. Perhaps you feel invisible—you're passed over for the promotion or never asked to lead the devotion at the bridal shower. Maybe you're friends with the most-liked person in the room, who gets gobs of attention and laughter while you're rarely invited into the conversation. Maybe you don't feel talented or attractive, wealthy or charismatic, memorable or desirable. You're the opposite of popular—you feel forgettable.

When I think about "forgettable" people, I think about the men, women, and children who participated in the story of redemption but never made it onto the pages of Scripture. While Moses is named more than 800 times, the remnant of faithful Israelites who followed him and helped to preserve the Word of God remain unnamed. While King David is mentioned more than 1,000 times, the individual followers of Yahweh who served under his reign are never scribbled into the scroll that told his story. In Scripture, some names are more popular than others—some get front-row coverage, some are in the back, and some can't be forgotten by us because they were never individually mentioned to us in the first place. For those who know the feeling of weakness that accompanies obscurity, this begs the question: Do mentions, recognition, and "front-row" status determine your worth in God's kingdom? Does "not mentioned" mean "not chosen" or "doesn't really matter"?

It's true: God gives some people great visible significance in the story of redemption. After all, stories have main characters, supporting characters, and (to our dismay) extras whose names don't make the end credits. But perhaps there's a way to forgo the feature role without drowning in obscurity, falling into self-pity, or tipping into despair. It's by knowing the main character and joyfully receiving the role we play in his story.

According to the Gospel of John, the star of God's story is Jesus Christ. He has works so numerous, so magnificent, so vast that "the world itself could not contain the books that would be written" about him. If you think you pale in comparison to the popularity and significance of your friends, family members, colleagues, and church community, imagine trying to stack yourself up to Jesus. His name has been spoken a gazillion times, and the count only increases.[1] He is the hero, the chosen one, the Lamb of God, the one worthy to open the scroll at the end of time to bring healing and judgment and renewal to the world. His name is mentioned more than Moses or David. He not only gets the starring role, he is the name above all names.

And though you're not the headliner of God's story and though you might exist in utter obscurity, if you have faith in Jesus, you are not overlooked. Your name has been called. You're noticed. You're chosen. Your name is written in the book of life. Your story matters to the one God is telling, even if it's lived in the back row. To him, you're unforgettable.

How do I know obscurity in this world doesn't mean obscurity to Jesus? Because the Gospels record a lifetime of Jesus seeing, calling, and valuing back-row kinds of people. Yes, he shared the gospel in synagogues and no doubt had some financially wealthy and well-known followers, but do you know where he spent quite a bit of his time during his public ministry? On mountains healing people with disease

---

1. You can thank my children for teaching me this vocabulary word, which means "a really, really big number."

and disability—the kinds of people high society avoided at all costs. Town after town, Jesus preached the gospel in ways that allowed the poor in spirit of every place in society to be comforted. Jesus noticed the destitute and uneducated, the sick and obscure.

If you have received Jesus's good news, you are his and he loves you. You have been seen. Your name has been called. You are remembered. You're in Christ's row. It's okay if you don't get the solo.

Additional Reading

> Matthew 15:29-31
>
> Revelation 5:1-5
>
> Ephesians 1:3-4

Questions for Reflection

I am weak

- In what areas of life do you feel unnoticed or overlooked?

- How does going unnoticed or overlooked in these areas impact your ability to function with joy and gratitude in daily life and relationships?

He is strong

- Where do you fit within God's story? Who is the main character, and how are you connected to him?

- How might knowing and being thankful that you're chosen by God in Christ change your response to the situations you listed above?

5

WHEN YOU NEED STRENGTII IN LIFE'S STORMS

*The rain fell, and the floods came, and the winds
blew and beat on that house, but it did not
fall, because it had been founded on the rock.*

MATTHEW 7:25

The day before my seventeenth birthday, I saw my first tornado. Our family was driving back home from a weekend at my grandparents' property in central Missouri when we encountered severe weather and saw a dark funnel swirling on the horizon. In the era before smartphones, there wasn't a good way to check the radar and see what was up ahead.

Instead, we listened intently to radio warnings and drove with caution as day turned to night. When we finally exited the freeway, we discussed what we might find in our neighborhood. Perhaps the storms had missed us.

But the lights flickered over the winding roads to our community, leaving an eerie sense of darkness. The storms hadn't missed us—they'd ripped a path right through. We did our best to weave through the wreckage, veering around downed trees and shielding our eyes from flashlights, floodlights, and emergency vehicles. People stood in the roads and in their yards, pointing out two-by-fours speared through garage doors and into formal dining rooms. Groups paced around and stared as we went by. On that strange and terrible drive, we saw the erratic nature of destruction. On the same street, some houses were untouched while others were leveled, oftentimes right next door to one another. In the coming weeks, as the damage was assessed and structures rebuilt, this was the lingering question— why did some houses stand and others fall?

At some point or another, everyone faces a storm. Whether the chaos and destruction descend from the clouds of betrayal, loss, sickness, disappointment, or persecution, or from trials of our own making, all of us endure circumstances that threaten to undo us. Why is it that when some people encounter a storm of suffering, death, false ideologies, or temptation, or the loss of a dream, they topple down a bottomless well of sorrow, bitterness, and resentment? But others—though they may find grief, confusion, scars, and questions leaking through the roof—ultimately weather life's storms. They even seem to come out on the other side with a stronger faith, wiser words, and brighter joy. What's the difference? Why do some people have the strength to stand?

In the Sermon on the Mount, Jesus talks about life's storms and identifies what causes a person to stand firm (Matthew 7:24-27). Maybe you can sing this parable, complete with hand motions! In case you need a refresher, the story has two main characters, a wise man and a foolish man. They each have a house. The wise man built his house on a rock, and when the storms came, his house stood firm. The foolish man built his house on sand, and when the storms came, his house went . . . *crash*. A simple image with a profound message about those who hear and obey Jesus: "Everyone then who hears these words of mine and does them will be like a wise man who built his house on the rock" (Matthew 7:24).

The wise man and the foolish man encountered the same storms, the same pounding winds, rain, and floods. But this is not an ancient version of the three little pigs. Nothing in the builder's choice of materials made the wise man's house stand firm. The strength of the structure was in the foundation, just as our ultimate strength is the result of a life built on Christ— even if still-standing houses are missing shingles and glass panes.

The storm imagery Jesus used would have made the original hearers think of the destruction of the flood in the days of Noah (Genesis 6:5-8). He meant for that to happen. Jesus is not just talking about how people stand firm in today's trials but how they stand firm through the final storm in the very end—when the earth is destroyed and remade and he comes to judge the living and the dead (2 Timothy 4:1; Revelation 22:12). How will we stand through *that* storm? As baptism illustrates, only those who come through the waters in the safety of their Savior Jesus Christ—their foundation—will stand for eternity with him.

Does something in your life today feel like a storm? Maybe shame from past sin rattles the shutters of your soul and threatens to rip you apart. Maybe the waters of grief from an ailing parent are rising and starting to pull you under. Maybe gossip, slander, or doubt pelt you like bullets of rain, and you're not sure how to keep going. But even as the winds of hurt howl, remember the security you're standing on. If you have built your life on Christ, you are loved and forgiven, embraced and comforted, known and justified. Eternally hopeful, forever secure. You're safe in the ark of Christ, able to feel the rain but safe from its destruction.

Though the houses in my community were built on the same type of foundation with the same materials and there was no clear explanation for why some stood through a tornado and others collapsed, in Jesus's parable the foundation determines the outcome. We build our lives on him by hearing God's Word and responding in faith. We build on the rock of Christ by abiding in him, knowing him, and clinging to his truth. You do not have to be so strong, but you do have to stand in the One who is.

⫸ Additional Reading ⫷

> Matthew 7:24-27
>
> Psalm 56:3-4
>
> Romans 8:37

⫸ Questions for Reflection ⫷

I am weak

- What storms of life, big or small, in the past or today, have threatened to undo you?
- In what ways do you feel weak and incapable of facing those storms? How are they affecting your life?

He is strong

- How does knowing your ultimate hope, strength, and security in Christ encourage you in life's storms?
- What action will you take today to run to, stand on, and cling to Christ as your rock in the midst of your trials?

—— 6 ——

WHEN YOU FEEL BAD AT LIFE

*For we are his workmanship, created in Christ
Jesus for good works, which God prepared
beforehand, that we should walk in them.*

EPHESIANS 2:10

After a long June day of free play and a bit too much screen time, I looked up from my phone and declared, "Wow, I'm being a slug today!" Even though I'd been working from my laptop, I couldn't really identify what I'd gotten done. I hadn't exercised like I planned or taken a shower. I remembered asking my oldest kids to start the laundry and clean their rooms, but *did they ever do that*? I didn't feel like making the bed, but I figured I probably should before dinner. I walked by the dishwasher, paused to look at the clean load, and kept walking. *I'll unload that later.* I knew the hours were slipping away faster than the pool days, but I couldn't seem to get enough fire under me to do something about it. In that moment, I longed to be a more naturally motivated, task-driven, productive person. Maybe that would make all of my responsibilities seem easier.

It's funny that I thought to use the word "slug" because while I imagined a sticky, slow-moving bug, it's also short for the word "sluggard," derived from a Norwegian word meaning "a large, heavy body."[1] My heart was enlarged and heavy with burdens. All of my responsibilities left me feeling stuck, overwhelmed, and paralyzed. The more I had to do, the slower I seemed to move.

Have you ever felt this way, having everything to do but feeling scattered and unmotivated to make progress on any of it? These feelings can be symptoms of a deeper struggle with issues like anxiety, depression, ADHD, or even a hormonal imbalance. They can also result from intense grief or trauma. So there are times when our sense of "blah" about facing hardships and getting things done has significant underlying concerns.[2] But other times, these feelings are just an unhelpful guest we invited in for an extended stay. It's not that we're going through a major life transition or need to see a licensed counselor; it's just that we're tired of having to try so hard. We're tired of facing obstacles in

---

1. Online Etymology Dictionary, s.v. "Sluggard," https://www.etymonline.com/word/sluggard.

2. If you think this might be you, please reach out to a medical professional or counselor. Sometimes the issue isn't primarily one of faith but of physiology.

everyday life, however small. We'd prefer for things to be easy and delightful, and we're not very resilient to roadblocks or failures. We want heaven now. (Ask me how I know.)

Sometimes I bemoan that I'm not naturally driven, self-disciplined, and intrinsically motivated. I grumble about those who seem to do life with excellence, ease, and perseverance. I whine about being "weaker" than people who don't have to try quite as hard to wake up early, stick to an exercise routine, keep their house picked up, or take care of their mounting inbox. What I really want to hear is "It's okay. That's just the way you are."

As I search the Scriptures, I see that yes, every person has different capacities, life circumstances, resources, gifts, and personalities. Some people are able to "do more" or have a bent toward accomplishment. Maybe due to their upbringing and the way they're wired, facing roadblocks, failures, or even just feeling tired doesn't cause them to plop onto the couch and give up. But while my personality and capacity might account for some of my frustrations with this type of weakness, deep down I know it's also about something else too. I harbor a flesh-fueled resistance to humbling myself before God, entrusting him with my needs, and believing he can help me do the good works he's prepared for me to do.

God doesn't want us to be "slugs." He wants us to be humble, hard workers who serve (Philippians 2:14-15; Colossians 3:23). He means for us to grow beyond spiritual infancy, into maturity (Ephesians 4:14-15). He doesn't want us to stay stuck in old habits or sin but to experience freedom and new life in Christ (2 Corinthians 3:17). To this end, we're to seek him with persistence and zeal (Isaiah 55:6-7). To seek help in hardship, fight sin, and not grow weary of doing good (Matthew 5:29; Galatians 6:9; Philippians 3:12; James 1:2-4).

This list can leave me feeling overwhelmed with conviction as I see my own inability to live according to these truths. *You too?* None of us are able to persevere in our own strength, and we constantly fall short of perfection. But God planned for our lack. Believers receive grace and walk by faith.

Faith is being so sure something is true that you're willing to take action, even if you can't see the outcome. In weakness, when your heart is enlarged and heavy with burdens, faith is believing you're a new creation and have the Spirit of God inside you to provide strength, direction, and help even if you don't immediately feel like it. Faith cries out to God for motivation to walk in good works—believing he has indeed prepared them for you, so they must be the better thing—even if that's simply moving toward the dishwasher and actually unloading it. Faith is being so convinced that you're being made new that you're willing to participate. Faith is praying for God to provide what you need to persist and then keeping your eyes peeled because you actually believe he will.

In our lack—of energy, motivation, self-discipline, perseverance, or fresh ideas—we can look to Christ's sufficiency and provision: "His divine power has granted to us all things that pertain to life and godliness" (2 Peter 1:3). In our need—of stronger desire and resources to serve with Christlikeness—we can have faith in God's promise: "He who did not spare his own Son but gave him up for us all, how will he not also with him graciously give us all things?" (Romans 8:32).

⟫⟫ Additional Reading ⟪⟪

Ephesians 2:1-10

2 Corinthians 5:17; Philippians 3:12

1 Peter 2:2-3, 9-12, 15-16

⟫⟫ Questions for Reflection ⟪⟪

I am weak

- Describe a time when you felt frustrated by your own weakness, especially if you compare yourself with people whom you consider to be "better" at life.

- What is underneath your frustration? In what ways are you struggling to have faith that God can help you grow and change?

He is strong

- In what areas of life do you need God's help to "walk in the good works" he has for you today? Write down specific areas where you're tired, frustrated, or unmotivated.

- When you face hardship or obstacles today, what verse or promise will you remember so you can approach the situation with faith?

7

WHEN YOU FEEL LIKE AN IMPOSTER

*He chose us in him before the foundation of the world,
that we should be holy and blameless before
him. In love he predestined us for adoption to
himself as sons through Jesus Christ, according to
the purpose of his will, to the praise of his glorious
grace, with which he has blessed us in the Beloved.*

EPHESIANS 1:4-6

I have a recurring dream where I'm fifteen and I'm riding in my parents' car to a dance competition. We have to stop the vehicle and turn back because I've forgotten my costume, my dance shoes, and a pair of earrings. Stress builds as I lug my almost-forgotten costume into the arena in a garment bag over my shoulder. I rush through my makeup in the green-room, panicking at the sight of empty vanity chairs, knowing my group is rehearsing without me. When I finally find my dance team, my teacher is frustrated. Everyone has been practicing; where have I been? I apologize and all seems well—that is, until the music starts.

The dream takes a strange turn when my limbs go wobbly. It's as if I've never lifted my leg into a graceful extension. I try to leap, but it feels like I'm wearing a weighted belt. I fall out of my turns, stumbling to land. And worst of all, I can't remember any of the choreography. Though I've presumably practiced the dance hundreds of times, the moves don't come to me, and I stand confused and exposed. As dreams do, it skips ahead, and I wait backstage for our group to be called back into the spotlight. I enter the lit stage with the sinking feeling that everyone in the crowd will see I don't know what I'm doing at all.

While your dream may differ, it's likely you've had a similar one at some point in your life. Whether a school exam or a public-speaking event, have you ever dreamt that you're up in front of others and you suddenly can't do what you hoped or promised? The feeling of embarrassment, fear, and paralysis when you need to perform is overwhelming. You feel like an imposter.

It's clearly not just the stuff of dreams. Imposter syndrome is said to be experienced by nearly 70 percent of people at some point in their lifetime.[1] It's a pop-psychology term that

---

1. Lydia Craig, "Are you suffering from imposter syndrome?" American Psychological Association, September 2018, https://www.apa.org/science /about/psa/2018/09/imposter-syndrome.

describes the "experience of feeling like a phony . . . as though at any moment you are going to be found out as a fraud—like you don't belong where you are, and you only got there through dumb luck."[2]

Imposter syndrome creeps into my own life as soon as I feel the warmth of another's gaze. I worry I'm an author who doesn't have helpful thoughts and can't actually write. Or that I'm a podcaster that speaks well behind a mic but can barely hold a conversation in person. That I'm the woman with a ministry for moms who isn't a very good mom herself. I worry I'm living a life I can't successfully execute and don't deserve. And just maybe I'll eventually be found out.

Have you ever felt this way? Like if people really knew you, they wouldn't give you any opportunities or awards? That you're not very good at your job or as kind as people say you are? That at any given point you're not going to be able to keep up appearances and you're going to let everyone down? While on the outside you appear strong and accomplished, spiritual and wise, or popular and platformed, inside you shiver with weakness.

When you carry around a sense of weakness about where you've arrived in life and live under the fear of being discovered as an imposter, it's important to remember that there's no such thing as "dumb luck." God does all that he pleases, and nothing in your life has happened by accident (Psalm 135:6). Any gifts, skills, talents, and opportunities are from the God who gives and takes away (Job 1:21; James 1:17). Additionally,

2. Arlin Cuncic, "What Is Imposter Syndrome?" Verywell Mind, July 27, 2022, https://www.verywellmind.com/imposter-syndrome-and-social-anxiety-disorder-4156469.

as you use your gifts as ministry in any capacity in your life, you're not held back or propelled by your own ability but by Christ (John 15:5). And while God distributes special gifts and talents, he's never been limited by them (Luke 1:37). You may feel weak in your skills or capacity to do the job, but in that gap, God's glory shines through (2 Corinthians 12:9).

Looping back to my dream—the one where I stand onstage and forget how to dance before a watching crowd— I have to ask myself, *So what?* What if that actually happened to me? What if your imposter fear became reality? What if you failed the test, bombed the big pitch meeting, or couldn't finish your painting? What if the person you discipled for a decade renounced Christ? Then what? There is deep comfort in knowing the outcome of your exposed weakness is still acceptance, identity, and security with your Father in heaven.

God didn't choose you because of your abilities. If you are in Christ, then before the foundation of the earth, your Creator loved, chose, and pursued you (Ephesians 1:4). Before you ever had any talent or won any awards or held a special job title, you were his. And even if your talents and gifts (given by him anyway) are stripped away, his you'll remain. Nothing is stripped from God, and Jesus Christ will still work through you.

It's helpful to know that no strength of your own brought you into the kingdom of God, so no lack of strength, intelligence, talent, productivity, or reputation will push you out. It's by grace, through faith, so that no one gets bragging rights. It's all Christ. It's up to us to receive his gifts and use them to delight in and serve our God.

⟫ Additional Reading ⟪

Ephesians 1:3-10

James 1:17

1 Peter 4:10

⟫ Questions for Reflection ⟪

I am weak

- Have you ever had a dream where you couldn't do what you were expected to do? What was the theme? Do you think it matches your fears about an aspect of your life?

- How does imposter syndrome leave you feeling weak? What are you afraid will happen if you are "found out" as not as good as others think you are?

He is strong

- What aspect of knowing you were chosen by God (Ephesians 1:3-10) gives you comfort and assurance, no matter what happens?

- How can you gain freedom in the face of imposter syndrome because of the reality of God's sovereignty and knowing you're just a steward of the gifts he gives?

8

WHEN YOU'RE OUT OF WILLPOWER

Peter said to him, "Even if I must die with you, I will not deny you!" And all the disciples said the same.

MATTHEW 26:35

A few years ago, I ran a 5K and promised myself I would not stop and walk. I knew the race would be harder on my mind than my lungs or my legs, and I was sure I could will myself to the finish line. I just had to forsake excuses and toughen up. But at the two-mile mark, someone offered me a cup of water, and the split-second slowdown overwhelmed me. I jogged a few feet when my pace broke, and my brain flooded with justifications to do what I said I wouldn't. The desire for a break won, and I walked.

The stakes were low for that last-minute promise to myself at a race, but this illustrates a pattern in my life. Have you noticed it in yours? There's the time I told myself I wouldn't eat all the cookies I baked the night before or that I'd make it through childbirth without an epidural. Or perhaps it's the times I've said I won't hit snooze in the morning or the sincere belief that I won't use a voice of frustration with my kids anymore. Time and time again, I've learned that telling myself to do something isn't a guarantee that I will actually do it.

I'm not the only human with a willpower problem. In the Gospels, Peter tells Jesus he won't deny him, even if it means he has to die. Peter is more confident than I was at my race; perhaps he even imagined himself being bound with Jesus and walking the road to Calvary. Peter had not only trained for this, he'd given his life to it. For three years he'd followed, learned from, sacrificed for, and loved Jesus. Seeing everyone turn against the one he'd followed all this time was Peter's moment to put his faith into action and prove his love. He would not let Jesus down, and neither would the other disciples.

But Jesus knew Peter better, and foretold how things would go: "Tonight all of you will fall away" (Matthew 26:31 CSB). Jesus knew his sheep would scatter when things got difficult. That evening started with a foreshadowing of their ultimate willpower breakdown. Jesus's closest friends arrived with him at the garden of Gethsemane confident they could stay awake and support him in prayer, but their word wasn't enough—only an hour later, Jesus found them asleep. In his darkest moment, when he needed them most, his closest friends couldn't even keep their eyes open.

This human response doesn't just reveal a lack of discipline or resilience. After all, some people do have more willpower than others and are able to withstand mounds of cookies without taking a bite. And for some, the urge to stop the race and walk just makes them run harder. But regardless of the strength or weakness of your word, regardless of your ability to grit your teeth and follow through to the end, this is still true: None of us would have stayed with Jesus. None of us, in Peter's or the other disciples' shoes, would have or could have taken the reproach that Jesus did. Only Jesus, God in the flesh, perfectly obeyed the Father's will to the point of death (Philippians 2:8). Only Jesus, God's Son, was the spotless lamb—the sacrifice for sin (1 Peter 1:19).

After Jesus's resurrection, he talks with Peter again. Peter was broken and repentant over his denial of Christ—he'd wept over his weakness and the worthlessness of his word to Jesus. And for every time that Peter uttered a betrayal of Jesus, Jesus gave him a chance to reaffirm his love. His reconciliation. His restoration. His new mission (John 21:17). As Peter went on to serve Christ's church, he "forgot" what lay behind and continued forward with a strengthened faith, as Paul talks about in Philippians 3:13.

This is an encouragement for you and me—who aren't as good as our word, who might not finish what we started or do exactly what we promised. We've betrayed our commitments, but what is even more concerning is we've often betrayed Christ and his commands.

Maybe you're frustrated with yourself because you said you'd pray more or start a daily Bible reading habit and the commitments just won't stick. Or maybe you're annoyed because you're still struggling with the same response to conflict, and no matter how many times you tell yourself that *next time* you'll believe the best and turn the other cheek, you need to repent again. Perhaps you told people you don't need help in your current circumstances, but you actually do.

In all this and more, the weakness of our will and our word isn't the end of the story, just as it wasn't the end of Peter's. It shouldn't surprise us when our strength falters, when we're overcome and choose to sit by the sidelines of our spiritual race. But in your weakness, you can turn to Jesus and receive the gift of grace. Tell him where you're struggling, and ask him for strength that you don't have. Seek his Word for wisdom, and ask him to hold you. We boast in Christ alone because we'd never make it by willpower alone.

⫸ Additional Reading ⫷

Matthew 26:30-75

John 21:15-19

Ephesians 2:8-9

⋙ *Questions for Reflection* ⋘

I am weak

- In what areas of life have you told yourself you'd do something? Why weren't you able to make good on that promise?

- In what ways have you shown that you're not able to perfectly obey and follow God, even today or this week? What does that reveal about your willpower against sin and need for a Savior?

He is strong

- What is your favorite part of the story of Peter and Jesus's relationship in Matthew 26 and John 21? How does this encourage you and give you confidence in your own relationship with Jesus?

- List all the ways you see Jesus's strength in these passages. Praise him for each one!

9

WHEN YOU'RE WAITING FOR SOMETHING

It is not for you to know times or seasons that the Father has fixed by his own authority.

ACTS 1:7

In the season of diagnosis, I spent weeks waiting for a phone call. Our son had undergone extensive genetic testing as doctors tried to pinpoint the reason for his developmental delays and give us a prognosis for his future. Anytime my phone rang, a jolt of adrenaline shot through my body as I checked my screen to see who it was. I even remember a "false alarm" in Aldi when his geneticist's office called to verify insurance while I was bagging groceries. I choked back tears as I pushed my cart out the door. That was not the call I was waiting for.

But the call did come. On a rainy summer day, I stood in my parents' kitchen before dinner, and when I answered the phone I was startled to hear the doctor's voice on the other end. *Why did he call directly? This must mean bad news.* He was kind and reassuring, experienced and compassionate, delivering just enough information to let us know he'd found something but not enough to let us take control and pull an all-nighter on Google. He asked us to come in the next morning.

After the kids were tucked into bed, I dragged a kitchen chair to our unfinished deck and watched the sunset. Tears rolled down my cheeks for the better part of an hour even though I didn't know what I was grieving quite yet. But after the call, I did know our journey had only started. I knew disability would become a permanent fixture in our family's life along with long seasons of waiting and not knowing, of having just enough information and not enough at the same time.

Sometimes when I read the Bible, I linger on moments of waiting. I imagine Noah and his family getting to the final stages of the ark, putting the finishing touches on the door and looking to the sky for even a single drop of rain. I hold my breath when I think of Abraham slowly raising his dagger into the air, wanting to hesitate but knowing he can't, feeling every heartbeat in slow motion. My chest tightens as I picture Moses standing at the edge of the Red Sea, swarmed by panicked Hebrews trying to flee as the threat closed in. *What was he thinking as he waited to see the first wave peel back?* Even in what each of these recipients of a miracle did see and experience—the flood, the ram, the dry ground—they were still people in waiting. And according to the writer of Hebrews, even though they each received a gift—shelter, protection, deliverance—they did not fully receive the promise they looked forward to (Hebrews 11:39).

The theme of waiting cascades into the New Testament. Jesus's disciples watched their resurrected Savior and helper—their hope and tangible surety of God's presence—rise off into the clouds. Before the ascension, Jesus told the disciples they wouldn't know when he would return to establish the kingdom on earth, but he followed up with the promise of an ever-present Helper, the Holy Spirit (Acts 1:4-8). That probably sounded comforting at the time, but I bet as Jesus floated away they had some follow-up questions. *Now what? How long will it be exactly before the promised Holy Spirit arrives? What are we supposed to be doing in the meantime?* They knew he would give help, but perhaps they wanted more information about the timing and the details. As they waited, they returned to Jerusalem, where they met together and devoted themselves to prayer (Acts 1:12-14). They continued with the work Christ had given them to do, replacing Judas with a new apostolic leader (Acts 1:15-20). They went along with observing the familiar days and traditions (Acts 2:1). And it was in the midst of these ordinary actions that God filled his people with the Spirit in his perfect timing (Acts 2:1-4). Today, we're all still waiting on the restoration of the kingdom the disciples asked about (Acts 1:6).

Are you familiar with waiting? Perhaps like me, it makes you feel weak and drives you to days or months of preoccupation as you check for updates. Maybe you're frustrated in your waiting, wanting to know more so you can do more—you can't stand the feeling of powerlessness that comes with not having all the information. Whether you're waiting on a call from a social worker, you've been on a long list to see a medical specialist, or you're longing for a wayward adult child to come to Christ, whether you're hoping for an apology from a friend or you're waiting to hear back from a potential employer—waiting feels like torture.

But God has given his people a paradigm for waiting. Just like the saints of old, you've experienced part of the promise, and you're waiting for its final fulfillment when Christ returns and makes all things new. Just like the early disciples had been told Jesus would send his Spirit but weren't sure when, you know Jesus is coming back a second time, but you don't know the day or the hour. The paradigm for waiting doesn't immediately eradicate the experience of waiting. And knowing that Jesus will one day make all things new doesn't magically turn the torturous waiting into a pesky inconvenience. But it does give us what we need to persist—certainty that God makes good on his promises. Our wait is not in vain.

In God's sovereignty and kindness, it is for our good that he asks us to wait. He gives limits to our knowledge and understanding. Yes, it drives us to heart-palpitating, adrenaline-shooting dependence on him in prayer, but it also propels us forward in everyday obedience because we have Christ, even when we don't have timelines. In our waiting, we put one foot in front of the other, doing the things we know to do as we wait on the Lord.

If you've already received and responded to the most important call to Christ, then you don't have to disdain the feeling of weakness and need in your waiting. We often want more knowledge and control, but God has given us all the information he wants us to have and the tools we need to trust him. It's not for us to know when the phone will ring or what news will be on the other side. Instead, we can pray, rejoice in who God is and the work he's already doing, be patient, look with hopeful anticipation for his provision, and believe that God is doing more than we can see. Get out of the bed and make it. Shop for groceries and cook meals. Make phone calls, fill out paperwork, and say prayers. He will give you the strength you need for what comes, whenever that may be.

➤➤ *Additional Reading* ◄◄

Acts 1

Psalm 27:13-14

Hebrews 11

⤞ *Questions for Reflection* ⤝

I am weak

- What is something you're waiting for in your life right now? How do you feel in the midst of your waiting? What is your experience of weakness as you wait?

- If you could get more information from God on your situation, what would you want to know? How is not knowing these things potentially helping you rely on him more in faith?

He is strong

- Why is God the best one to decide the timing and outcome of events and the details we should know along the way?

- What actions will you take today in the midst of your waiting to show your faith in God and hope in the truth of his ultimate promises in Christ?

10

WHEN YOU'RE EXHAUSTED BY GRIEF

My eyes have grown dim from grief, and my whole body has become but a shadow.

JOB 17:7 CSB

I've often struggled to understand how a one-hour doctor's appointment can consume my whole day. First, there is the anticipation: *What will we hear? Will there be new tests, concerns, or medications? Will our son be happy, or will the day be full of crying and frustration?* Then there's the forty-five-minute commute, the unknown period of time in the waiting room, the letdown on the drive home, and the reporting back to friends and family. What looks like a tiny rectangle on my Google Calendar leads to a twenty-four-hour period of exhaustion.

Even if I hear good news, I know I'll feel physically tired, want to order pizza for dinner, and struggle to do more than stare at a screen.

Especially in the early years of our son's diagnosis and follow-up appointments, this phenomenon troubled me. I beat myself up and felt guilty for not instantly engaging a household of children when I returned home. For letting one hour hijack a day's worth of productivity. But eventually, I realized these weren't symptoms of laziness but of grief. Though subconscious, "appointment day" intensified the loss and pain of disability. It was a weighted blanket on my energy levels and a barrier between my heart and everyday life. Even when I prayed, rejoiced, gave thanks, and experienced God's provision and presence in the midst of it, these days were hard. They still are.

Maybe you grieve more deeply and for different reasons, but have you also felt weak in the midst of it? Could you almost echo the words of Job—feeling your whole body has become but a shadow (Job 17:7)? You're not alone. Scientists say that grief isn't just an emotional experience: It affects the body too.[1] Impaired immune function, insomnia, sleep disturbance, appetite changes, gray hair, high blood pressure, chest pain, fatigue, inflammation, and joint pain are just a few of the symptoms commonly associated with grief. And for those

---

1. Carmelita Swiner, "How Grief Can Affect Your Health," WebMD, June 29, 2021, https://www.webmd.com/mental-health/ss/slideshow-grief-health-effects; Mary-Frances O'Connor, "Grief: A Brief History on How Body, Mind, and Brain Adapt," *Psychosomatic Medicine* 81, no. 8 (October 2019): 731–738, https://www.ncbi.nlm.nih.gov/pmc/articles/PMC6844541/.

who want to avoid processing grief altogether, a myriad of medical issues await.[2] It's no surprise that we feel like a dim version of ourselves when we're betrayed, bereaved, sinned against, or when we experience deep disappointment.

For me, the feeling of weakness heaps grief upon grief—I'm not only sorrowful about the original thing but also sad and frustrated with my response. My inability and feeling of uselessness make the situation even more maddening. This multiplied grief is where I need to pause. Should I feel guilt over the weakness of my mourning?

In Isaiah's prophecy, God's people get an unexpected image of their Messiah. Instead of a word picture of a Savior beaming with smiles on the path to success and political domination, we read of a man of sorrows, acquainted with grief, taking the path to death. A man despised, rejected, afflicted, oppressed, and crushed. This was God's will for his beloved Son, for Jesus to bear our iniquities to make many righteous (Isaiah 53).

Isaiah's prophecy came to fruition. Jesus was a man of sorrows. He wept, bore burdens, and mourned over sin. Though he certainly enjoyed the Father's good gifts during his time on earth, his life was still characterized by grief. And since he experienced grief in a human body, he must have also experienced some of its symptoms (Hebrews 4:15). Was Jesus pitiful because of his grief? Certainly not. Jesus's grief was the perfect response

---

2. Neha Pathak, "How Grief Shows Up in Your Body," WebMD, July 11, 2019, https://www.webmd.com/special-reports/grief-stages/20190711 /how-grief-affects-your-body-and-mind.

to his encounters with death, sin, and the havoc the fall wreaked on God's perfect creation (Genesis 1; John 1).

You and I are not Jesus, so we are prone to let our grief tip into bitterness and self-pity. We can err in our sadness and get stuck in a loop of rumination. Our grief is tainted by the very fall that brought our heartbreaking circumstances about. But grief itself and its immediate effects are not a type of weakness to be ashamed of. We should grieve toward God—pouring out our complaints to him and telling him our troubles (Psalm 142:2).[3]

In your grief today—whether over the loss of a parent or spouse, a dream or job, whether from childhood trauma or last night's argument with your husband—know that it's normal to feel tired and weak. The question is not whether our grief will affect us but whether our grief will cause us to more deeply depend on our compassionate and steadfast God. We can wait with hope for the day when our tears will be wiped away and let that hope bring us shreds of comfort in today's hard things.

---

3. I once heard my friend and sister-in-law, Laura Wifler, use the phrase "doubt toward God" and thought it was a great way to describe our posture in grief as well. This is a spin-off of her wisdom!

⟫ **Additional Reading** ⟪

Isaiah 53

Hebrews 4:15-16

Romans 15:13

⟫ **Questions for Reflection** ⟪

I am weak

- In what ways does grief make you feel weak?
- How do you typically respond when you experience these feelings or symptoms?

He is strong

- How does knowing Jesus was "a man of sorrows, acquainted with grief" change the way you view your own grief?
- What would it look like to grieve toward God and hold on to hope in the midst of your grief today? How might it help you continue to love God and others in the midst of your pain?

11

WHEN YOU NEED MINUTE-BY-MINUTE STRENGTH

We rejoice in our sufferings, knowing that suffering produces endurance, and endurance produces character, and character produces hope, and hope does not put us to shame.

ROMANS 5:3-5

Light peeked through the blinds and landed on the hospital recliner chair, waking me from a stiff-necked sleep. I turned my head to see my five-year-old son, curled up in a ball with monitors beeping steadily, feeling sure it would only be a few minutes before he sensed me and woke up. We had at least another day ahead of us in this specially sectioned-off unit—not allowed to leave the room or accept visitors. Nurses or doctors would only drop in on an as-needed basis. While I praised God that my son had been stable through the night, my prayers now shifted to the daytime. How would I entertain him in this sterile room for hours on end? How could I explain to him that we couldn't leave or unhook his cords? I sat up, called for breakfast, and looked through my small bag of toys. This was going to be a long day.

My son has intellectual disability, is nonspeaking, and struggles with new environments and situations. After waking, he immediately reached through the crib and pointed to my lap, his haven of safety. It was evident from the face smacking and hair pulling (however affectionate) that he did not want to be in this room one minute longer, and thus the marathon began. I rotated the few items I had—playing ball, pressing light-up buttons, flipping through board books. Seven minutes passed. We started to FaceTime any family member who was awake, but soon my phone battery drained to nothing. *It's not even 10:00 am!* I plugged in my phone so we could watch Pete the Cat on repeat from an awkward angle in the recliner. *It's 10:09.* I realized we were going to get through this day one minute at a time. Three hundred and sixty minutes passed before we were released and collapsed into the care of my husband. And during almost every single one of those minutes, I prayed: "Lord, help sustain us—give us endurance and patience for one more minute."

Have there been moments or seasons in your life when you needed extraordinary endurance? When you weren't sure how you'd make it one more minute? Your patience had run dry, resistance to temptation had worn thin, and your words of wisdom neared zero. I have rarely felt the need for endurance as acutely as I did in that hospital room, but I've experienced the feeling of being near empty many times. Having to stay up late, wake up early, or bottle energy to care for an aging or disabled family member can deplete you. Or perhaps you're exhausted by managing the ongoing needs of a household and family. But often it's in this struggle when the good stuff happens.

The author of Hebrews tells us that if we're weary or fainthearted, we should consider Jesus and look to him for strength. Jesus is the perfect example of endurance because he experienced the strongest suffering without giving up—not because he was a glutton for punishment but because he trusted his Father, even unto death. While we don't have a detailed account of what was going through our Savior's mind, perhaps his prayer in Gethsemane and the drops of blood that fell like sweat from his brow point to his minute-by-minute, second-by-second need for endurance as he was beaten, mocked, and hung to suffocate on the cross (Matthew 26:38-39). He received the bonds and the blows because of an iron-clad trust in his Father's good plan (Hebrews 12:2-3). Jesus's suffering didn't get the last word, and his hope didn't put him to shame. His Father made good on every promise—Jesus walked out of the tomb, ascended to heaven, and sits at the Father's right hand.

In our suffering, when we feel weak and desperate for endurance, we are walking the path to hope in God. As your teenage child gets on your last nerve, as you drive one more day to a job you can't stand, as you sit beside your ailing, unappreciative, aging parent, as you continue to share the gospel where it's not yet received, you can endure because you have hope.

Hope says . . .
God is with me.
God will help me.
What I see is not all that's happening.
This suffering will not last forever.

Just as surely as you know the sun will rise and gravity will keep you from floating off into space, know that your hope in God will not put you to shame. Our hope is as secure as our salvation because all of God's promises hold true. He will do all that he says—as surely as he raised Jesus from the dead, he will eventually bring you to his side. He is the firstfruits and we are the future harvest (1 Corinthians 15:20).

While you might feel desperately weak, needing minute-by-minute strength to endure what the Lord has given you to do, you are not alone. You are not unseen. You are not unequipped. Tell the Lord that you need his help to keep going and then watch with undeserved amazement as minute by minute he lifts your drooping hands and strengthens your weak knees (Job 4:4; Hebrews 12:12). This might be a long day, week, year, or decade, but God will see you through to the end one moment at a time.

≫ Additional Reading ≪

Hebrews 12:1-4

Psalm 37:5-6

Psalm 42:5

≫ Questions for Reflection ≪

I am weak

- In what area(s) of life do you feel worn down and in need of endurance?

- Which of your resources are specifically depleted (patience, physical strength, ideas, or even hope)?

He is strong

- How does hope in God change how you respond and move forward when you need endurance? In your own life, what does hope "say," and what would it look like?

- How does the resurrection of Christ give you hope and confidence in the midst of your current struggle or suffering?

12

WHEN YOU NEED COMPASSION

We urge you, brothers, admonish the idle, encourage the fainthearted, help the weak, be patient with them all.

1 THESSALONIANS 5:14

I was posing for a group picture under the dim glow of downtown lights, laughing with a crowd of old and new friends, when I spotted her. "Three, two, one, smile!" The photo snapped, and I gave a quick grin before my eyes flitted back to her again. *Yes, she is definitely crying.* My heart began to beat quickly as the group stood up from the fountain, congregating to talk and head off to the ice cream shop down the street. I kept stealing glances. *She's not just crying, she's sobbing. Is she alone?* Not being able to stand it anymore, compassion ripped me away from the group and gave my feet courage to approach a stranger in the dark.

Nearly fifteen years have passed since that moment, and I can't remember her name or her words. But I remember hugging her. Praying for her. Feeling a strange connection to this other human who'd experienced the type of undoing that I'd been through myself. I remember that her tears didn't repulse me, they drew me in.

I can think of others whose weakness and need tug me with an invisible string. A dear friend, disabled by decades of sexual abuse, living a faithful and godly life as she struggles with the long-term effects of complex PTSD. She relies on the care and support of the church body as she goes through counseling and pays her bills. My son, who can't use words to tell me that his stomach or his head hurts—who as a young boy must rely on others to feed him, transport him, and change his soiled diapers—who without provision and protection from others would perish. When I think of them, I'm not put off by weakness, repelled and disgusted. Christ in me—the Spirit in me—pulls me closer to them to encourage and protect. As I see their struggles, I have supernatural patience and consider it a blessing to serve and love them.

But what about when it comes to my own struggles, weaknesses, and needs? When I am the one who is frail and faint-hearted, teary-eyed and in need of prayer? Or what about when you need those things? Maybe when it comes to having compassion and patience with others in their weakness, you're quick to step in and serve, but when it comes to your own weakness, you jump straight to self-berating. Pride whispers,

Get your act together and stop being ridiculous. You can figure this out. Don't accept help, and certainly don't ask for it.

In the first letter to the Thessalonian church, Paul and Timothy describe groups of people to be patient with—giving actions to correspond with various struggles (1 Thessalonians 5:14). Some people in the body are struggling with idleness, refusing to do necessary work because they say they are waiting for the Lord to come back any day. Paul says this group should be admonished or warned of the consequences of their inaction. They ought to keep working and provide for themselves and their families while they wait. But others aren't idle; they are fainthearted. Said another way, they are small-souled, little-spirited, fretful, discouraged, despondent, and feeling despair.[1] Like the woman I saw sobbing downtown, they've come face-to-face with sin and tragedy, and they are struggling to keep the faith in the midst of it. Paul says the church (which includes you and me) ought to encourage them in the midst of their grief.

Finally, he addresses the weak. Some Bible translations use the word "infirm" because this alludes to those who have some type of physical or bodily limitation that renders them vulnerable and helpless. For this group, the church is to help them—covering them, protecting them, sustaining them, and supporting their life. In all of this, Paul responds not with annoyance and disdain, eye-rolling or a "get-your-act-together" attitude, but with a call to a posture of patience—the gentle, provisional, protective posture Christ has toward his sheep (Isaiah 40:11).

---

1. These terms are from "1 Thessalonians 5:14-15 Commentary," Precept Austin, April 28, 2020, https://www.preceptaustin.org/1thessalonians_514-15.

Our Spirit-fueled impulse to care for and come alongside others in weakness—either self-imposed or due to causes out of their control—is good and loving. It matches Paul's famous passage on love in 1 Corinthians 13, where he describes Christian love as patient and kind. But sometimes we have to recognize that we are the fainthearted and weak, that we are in need of encouragement, help, and patience from others. Sometimes you're the one who is battling depression, laid up on bed rest, unexpectedly widowed, chronically ill, or in the early phases of Alzheimer's. Sometimes you're the one weeping and helpless. Sometimes you need the body of Christ to be patient with you.

In these moments, what will you do? Will you remember your love and compassion for others and give the church the gift of acting in compassion toward you, receiving their love with grace and appreciation? Or will you hole up in pride and self-sufficiency?

It wouldn't be your first time to be counted worthy of compassion. While we were still weak, at just the right time, Christ died for us (Romans 5:6). He didn't recoil, he came near. He didn't tell us to fix it, he entered in with a solution. He didn't leave us to ourselves, he brought us to himself. The compassion of Christ can draw you into compassion for yourself and push you out in compassion toward others.

⫸ Additional Reading ⫷

 Romans 5:6-9

 Psalm 23

 Matthew 9:36

⫸ Questions for Reflection ⫷

I am weak

- Can you think of a time you were compelled by compassion for someone's weakness?

- What areas of weakness (such as of heart, mind, body, or spirit) do you experience? In these, are you hard on yourself or slow to ask for help?

He is strong

- Reflecting on Matthew 9:36, how does Jesus's compassion impact you? How does it impact your posture toward others?

- Thinking of Psalm 23, what would it look like to entrust yourself to the Lord as your good shepherd today? What might he do for you in the midst of your struggle?

13

WHEN YOU'RE TIRED OF BEING SICK

So we do not lose heart. Though our outer self is wasting away, our inner self is being renewed day by day.

2 CORINTHIANS 4:16

I shuffled between the bed, the living room chair, and the couch, leaving a growing pile of tissues at every stop. On the first morning of being sick, I felt a little dizzy, but by the next evening, I shuddered in bed with chills, fever, and body aches. Even when that subsided, I was still too fatigued and congested to help with anything or anyone around the house. Instead of pitching in, I watched my husband fold a mountain of laundry and make frozen pizza for the kids. Even though he was happy to serve, I still felt bad being isolated—for needing so much help.

When I'm going through bouts of illness, it's not lost on me that some people struggle with fatigue and pain on a regular basis. Maybe this is you. Maybe you live with challenging symptoms on a daily basis because of an autoimmune disease, chronic pain, persistent digestive issues, insomnia, cancer, migraines, a not-yet-diagnosed condition, or lingering effects from an injury or surgery. Even if it's not daily, perhaps occasional weeks-long flare-ups wreak havoc on your work schedule and family life. Maybe it's frustrating and hard for you to know when you'll be feeling well and full of energy or need extra time off to rest. And it's even harder to explain it to others.

When I was sick, one of my children plopped down on the couch and said, "Mom, you're looking at your phone too much. Why don't you read a book or something? When are you going to be better?" I tried to explain how reading made my head hurt and I could barely retain information, so staring at my phone felt like all I could do. But I could tell he didn't understand. *I was sitting in the living room. I looked like the same mom. Why couldn't I act like her and snap out of it?* It struck me that in moments of pain, illness, or fatigue, it can also be disheartening when others may not understand what we're feeling or perhaps don't even believe that we're really in pain. This leaves you further frustrated and distressed. In the midst of this experience of weakness, what hope is available?

Throughout the Bible, God frequently addresses physical illness, disease, and pain. As part of life after the fall, a consequence of Adam and Eve's sin and the reality of death, these "jars of clay" that we embody as image-bearers are not only limited (a good function of God's design), but they are wasting away. And even if we feel healthy today, eventually old age will come for us all.

If you live with a chronic feeling of "wasting away," shuddering at that phrase as you feel it in your body today, Paul gives you a reason to hope. And interestingly, it begins with acknowledging and validating the reality of sickness and pain. Translated another way, "wasting" is a word picture of something decaying. Most of us don't look at our bodies and see what will eventually be a rotting corpse, but we ought to remember that our bodies are destined for a grave. You're not imagining your pain or fatigue. It is real, and Paul acknowledges that in some way, shape, or form, it's part of every human life until Christ returns.

But while your body is wasting away, there is part of you that is not. Paul calls it the "inner self." The same expression is used in Ephesians 3:16-17 when Paul speaks of God's Spirit living inside believers. Because God is eternal, never fading, wasting away, decaying, or dying, this part of us that is "born again" is actually being renewed. Your digestive system might be causing you cramps, but the Spirit of Christ in you is not keeled over. You might be in bed with a migraine, but the Spirit of Christ in you is not laid up. You may wince at each twist of your wrist and bend at your joints, but the Spirit of Christ in you is not incapacitated. Christ in you is healthy, whole, and strong.

Ultimately, this is why you don't lose heart—though you can see the braces, the medications and supplements, the outline of your body in the bed, the medical charts, and the mounting bills, these seen things are not your final and full reality. Jesus said, "I am the resurrection and the life. Whoever believes in me, though he die, yet shall he live" (John 11:25). If you believe in him, your body will go to a grave, but it's not stuck there. God will raise you up by his power and give your physical body life again, free from pain or illness (1 Corinthians 6:14).

In the meantime, because your inner self is being renewed and a piece of eternal life lives in you today, even while lying, resting, recovering, or being hooked up to machines, you are needed for kingdom work. You are able to display God's glory. This is going to look different based on the limitations you experience, but it's worth considering. As part of God's family and as a citizen in his kingdom, you have been chosen as a vessel of his glory to tell his story. Whether through prayer, rejoicing, or just radical joy in the face of hard things, you can encourage other believers and be a testimony of resurrection hope.

In this life we will waste away. We will need help. Not everyone will understand our pain. But the Spirit in us is strong and has a chance to glow brighter than ever. For your "light momentary affliction is preparing for [you] an eternal weight of glory beyond all comparison" (2 Corinthians 4:17).

⤜ Additional Reading ⤛

2 Corinthians 4:7-18

Romans 8:11

Philippians 2:13

≫ *Questions for Reflection* ≪

I am weak

- What physical ailments are you facing today? If nothing comes to mind, spend a few minutes imagining what it might be like to live with chronic disease, pain, or even just the effects of aging.

- In the midst of your physical weakness, what parts are particularly frustrating and limiting? In what ways do you feel limited in your ability to love God and serve others in the way you expected or desired?

He is strong

- How does knowing God's Spirit is being renewed in you change your perspective on your usefulness or ability to give glory to God today?

- How does knowing the temporary nature of your illness or pain give you hope today and joy in who Christ is and what he's done or will do?

14

WHEN YOUR MIND IS FADING

I am sure of this, that he who began a good work in you
will bring it to completion at the day of Jesus Christ.

PHILIPPIANS 1:6

My mother-in-law, Dianne, met her friend Grace in college. They were part of the same campus ministry, and after leaving school and getting married, they stayed long-distance friends through life's ups and downs—cross-country moves, raising children, empty nesting. Then in her fifties, Grace was diagnosed with an aggressive form of Parkinson's disease. Today, it has progressed to its late stages, and she struggles with mobility, persistent fatigue, personality changes, and memory loss. Every week, Dianne faithfully calls Grace on

Zoom and reads her a selection from a children's story Bible. Even though Grace struggles to remember her family members and the details of her condition, as a believer she is comforted by the simple truths of the gospel. Sometimes Dianne also prays, recites Bible verses, and sings hymns to her. As Grace struggles to hold on to her mind, God's grace holds on to her.

Just as my mother-in-law, Dianne, marvels at the Spirit's ongoing work in her friend Grace, I've marveled at it in the lives of others. My maternal grandfather, a former Baptist pastor, was cognitively debilitated in his fifties by multiple strokes. Even so, he continued to love his family, listen to hymns, pray, and treasure the Bible to the end of his life. My adult brother with intellectual disability faithfully attends church and highlights portions of his Bible despite his challenges with reading and communication. In these cases, cognitive changes made aspects of life difficult, but they didn't preclude sincere faith.

Today, you may enjoy the benefits of a working memory and a brain that can string sentences together. Maybe you can still recount memories of your spouse and children, do a quick math problem in your head, and brainstorm solutions in a tough situation. But this might not always be the case. Whether from disease, an unexpected injury, or aging, at some point these skills will fade because your outer self is "wasting away." You'll change. Do you ever imagine how powerless or even terrified you might feel to discover your mental ability is slipping?

Or perhaps you've been diagnosed and are in the early

stages of Alzheimer's. Maybe a disease of early cognitive decline runs in your family and it's only a matter of years before it could happen to you. Maybe you have intellectual disabilities or cognitive impairments that make it difficult to read and process information. Words and phrases slip from your mind or come out in unintended ways. You have lapses in memory or judgment. In this case, a dimming mind is already your reality, and you're familiar with this type of weakness.

Regardless of where you're at on the spectrum of memory, intelligence, or cognition, there's a sure promise that won't slip or fade, even if you do. In Paul's letter to the church in Philippi, he mentions this promise to believers: God won't leave his work unfinished. Regardless of what persecution or struggle awaits the Philippian Christians, Paul is confident that God will keep hold of them and ultimately make them like Jesus when he returns. Though this promise isn't particularly said in the context of cognitive ability or aging, taken in the greater context of Scripture, it applies. Consider Romans 8:31-39, for example, where Paul details numerous things that could seemingly "threaten" our ability to be loved by and unified with Christ. If destitution, demons, danger, or even death can't separate us from the love of God, then surely a fading memory won't do it either. Our bond to God in Christ is unbreakable.

True faith is not contingent on IQ, age level, or stage of life. You don't have to remember your own name to have the Spirit inside you. Though you may lose the ability to drive or talk, though you may not be able to feed yourself or take yourself to the restroom, though the point may come when you stutter or stumble or become a shadow of who you once were—Christ promises not to let you go when you're no longer "useful" by the world's standards. The weakness of the mind is only temporary.

What Christ starts, he finishes. What Christ gains, he keeps. Jesus loves you, and his grace will keep you all the way.

➤➤➤ Additional Reading ◀◀◀

> Romans 8:31-39
>
> John 10:27-28
>
> 2 Corinthians 4:16

➤➤➤ Questions for Reflection ◀◀◀

I am weak

- Have you experienced or imagined what it would be like to lose some of your mental abilities or have a change in your memory or cognition? What type of impact would this (or does this) have on your life?

- What fears might you (or do you) experience about your faith and your usefulness in God's kingdom if you don't have peak mental capacity?

He is strong

- Looking back over the list of things that can't separate you from God in Christ in Romans 8:31-39, which ones are most encouraging to you? If God is able to keep you through those, do you think he can keep you through cognitive changes? Why or why not?

- How does knowing that Christ keeps and values you, regardless of your cognitive abilities, give you a sense of deep hope and security?

15

WHEN YOU'RE SUPER TIRED

*I lay down and slept; I woke again, for
the LORD sustained me.*

PSALM 3:5

By day three, my nerves were shot. My husband and I had spent multiple nights taking turns comforting our son with disabilities through frequent night wakings and even a seizure. The thought of his cry or moan becoming a medical emergency meant that any sleep I did get was light and laced with adrenaline. While I'd held myself together with coffee, a smile, and a repeated reminder that this was just a blip on the radar of life, after seventy-two hours with little sleep and a lot of worry, I was struggling. Loud noises from my children or the slam of the back door made me cringe and jump. I felt less able to regulate my tone of voice in conflict and was quick to turn on the TV for the kids instead of finding something else for them to do. Though I went through the motions of my workout, I lifted light and struggled to perform with my usual energy. Things that I could typically process rationally left me feeling anxious and overwhelmed. Sleep deprivation was getting to me.

As I made the bed, I thought of all the nights of solid sleep I'd gotten before and felt upset that I'd taken it for granted. In the days of having five kids age five and under, I had lived in a constant sleepy daze, but now, going from well-rested to sleep-deprived in a matter of days made the effects too clear to miss. Enough rest gave me endurance, creativity, willpower, and mental clarity—a strength I didn't realize I'd had. Without rest, the pieces of life were hard to hold together, daily activities were difficult to complete, questions were hard to answer, everyday problems were intimidating to solve. It was easy to eat half a bag of chips in one sitting and nearly impossible to get out of bed before the kids to shower and read my Bible. How much of my day-to-day performance had been held together by adequate sleep?

In the midst of our endless days, I was quick to scold myself for falling behind. Quick to tell myself that no one cared if I didn't sleep well. *Don't have a pity party. Get to work!* But my internal monologue didn't help. Now I was tired *and* ashamed of being tired.

While having a child with epilepsy might not keep you

up at night, does something else disrupt your rest? Phone calls from your parent's nursing home or hospice center. Late-night texts or lack of texts from your teenager. Unexplained insomnia and sleep disturbances. Nursing babies or comforting a toddler with an ear infection. A household with a stomach bug. Whether the deprivation goes on for days, weeks, or years, most people are familiar with the feeling of going without adequate sleep.

The weakness you feel in this state is not imagined. Sleep is as necessary to daily survival as your heart beating and your lungs breathing—like water or food. It isn't a "nice to have" if you're able. Sleep impacts nearly every system of the body. God designed us to need rest. He made it a requirement for our rejuvenation and function. We sleep so that we can process and retain memories, learn new skills, build muscles, regulate emotional health, digest food, repair injuries, fight viruses, and more.[1]

In some ways, the need to sleep for at least 30 percent of our day does put us in a state of repetitive weakness. Without a shelter or safety, it's a time of day when we're vulnerable, open to attack or injury. That's why the book of Psalms talks about the need for watchmen, those who stay awake in shifts so that others can sleep in safety (Psalm 130:5-6). Sleep is one of many things that differentiate us from God, who is always watching and working, never needing to slumber or sleep as we rely on him (Psalm 121:4).

---

1. Raj Dasgupta, "What Is the Purpose of Sleep?" Healthline, July 20, 2020, https://www.healthline.com/health/why-do-we-sleep#what-happens-during-sleep.

But in the moral sense, needing seven to nine hours of sleep doesn't make our character "weak" or less than. It leaves us strong and ready for another day. Jesus, God born in the likeness of man, slept (Philippians 2:7). Jesus, who never sinned or erred or disobeyed his Father, allowed himself to be "weak" in this way. Even more, Jesus also endured and experienced sleep deprivation for the sake of service. There were times when the presence of his disciples or the sick and needy crowds meant that he didn't get the ideal amount of sleep for his body. He woke up early to go away by himself and be alone with God. He stayed up in the garden before his arrest and crucifixion to pray and submit himself fully to the Father in the midst of horribly trying circumstances. Though sleep was crucial, it was not his sole sustenance.

I think about these things as I shuffle around the house wishing I wasn't so frazzled. I observe how my life seems to be a few good nights' sleep away from crumbling, but God is still Lord.

In the midst of sleep deprivation, you don't have to give yourself a hard time. Its effects are real. You also don't have to give yourself a hard time for protecting and prioritizing sleep, a God-created need in your life. Neither of these things makes you "weak" in the kind of way that a military general or a hyperproductive, get-it-done-at-any-cost type of person might make it sound.

Though we feel weakened and humbled, looking forward to a day of ultimate and final rest, God is never tired, and he will see us through.

⫸ Additional Reading ⫷

Psalm 3:3-6

Mark 4:37-39

Psalm 54:4

⫸ Questions for Reflection ⫷

I am weak

- Can you think of a time when you were tired and sleep-deprived? How did that affect you and your life?

- How are sleeping and not getting enough sleep both forms of weakness? Which one frustrates you more?

He is strong

- How are you encouraged by the fact that Jesus both needed sleep and experienced the feeling of exhaustion?

- What aspects of your life and perspective would change if you believed that God never slumbers or sleeps and that he sustains your life?

16

WHEN YOU FEEL LIKE
A LOW ACHIEVER

His master said to him, "Well done, good and faithful
servant. You have been faithful over a little; I will set
you over much. Enter into the joy of your master."

MATTHEW 25:23

The week between Christmas and New Year's Day is supposed to be the most relaxing week of the year—the one when you're allowed to do nothing. If you do choose to do something, it should involve friends, family, food, and loungewear. But in between high-carb snacks and board games, when you tuck your sock feet under your sweatpants and curl up to check your phone, reality sets in. This is also the week your friends, family, and favorite influencers report all they accomplished in the last year. Book lists abound: "I read every night! Here's my full list . . ." Humble brags are abundant: "I'm so #blessed by the success of my business." And annual highlight reels fill our feed: "We went on four family trips, planted a garden, remodeled a house, bought a dog, paid off our debt, and overhauled our diet this year!"

Tucked into my couch, I'm tempted to immediately scoff and give a side-eye. But while it can be tough to watch others count their blessings, I need to remember that it glorifies God when people acknowledge the gifts he's given, mark milestones, and celebrate. It's good to have aspirations, consider how to grow and cultivate resources, and yes, recount progress. But for those of us who aren't superachievers (by whatever definition or measure of comparison you use) or who are exhausted by the pressure to do-do-do and prove-prove-prove, the reminders of others' wins fill "the most relaxing week of the year" with fresh anxiety. One minute you're sitting in sweatpants enjoying a movie night with your kids, and the next minute you're spiraling in self-condemnation because your booklist for the year is only four books long instead of forty-four. And you haven't even thought about next year's Bible reading plan or crafted something inspirational to post on social media about your goals.

Perhaps this is frustrating not because of your personality or preferences but because the Lord has you in a season where you're just trying to accomplish the basics. Maybe the past months or years have been spent battling depression or the ongoing impacts of childhood trauma. Maybe you've just relocated, started a new job, transitioned into motherhood, or are working to heal a relationship. Maybe the budget is tight and you're spending as much time as possible trying to make ends meet. Maybe due to chronic pain or the impacts of aging, your energy and window to accomplish things are unpredictable or growing smaller each year.

Have you felt the pressure and anxiety of feeling "less than" compared to someone else? Everyone desires to do good things and hear "job well done." Through likes and compliments on a social media post, public accolades and awards, or just the feeling of crossing something off our bucket list, we want to know we're measuring up. To know our life and efforts matter, and point to specific outcomes to prove it.

In the parable of the talents, Jesus talks about the nature of accomplishment and what constitutes a faithful servant. The master doesn't give the servants the same amount to start out with, but despite the uneven amounts, there is no extra value implied or glory to be had the way it is distributed. It's simply given according to the master's wisdom and knowledge of each recipient. Similarly, God gives each of us different seasons, circumstances, and abilities, different interests, capacities, and resources. Our "talents" vary, and because of this, the nature of our achievements will vary. If God has given you a medically complex child to care for on a daily basis, perhaps faithfulness looks like giving medication on time or making sure your child gets to their appointments. Maybe it's dignifying their life by praying over them and reading to them, even if they can't respond.

We also see that the first faithful servant "went at once" and began to steward what the master gave him. The servant with two talents also responded in obedience, doubling what the master gave him to make two talents more. But the unfaithful servant hesitated, doubted, and feared—resulting in no multiplication of resources. He achieved nothing.

The nature of faithfulness is measured by obedient stewardship of what God has given *you*. If God has given you a house full of young children, that day or year's accomplishments will look different from your friend who is finishing her dissertation. Your accomplishments might be loving your children with patience, serving with diligence, feeding them repeatedly, and nursing their boo-boos. Does the fact that you have no grade or big goal to check off after a long day with kids mean you haven't actively stewarded what God has given you?

When it comes to achievements and showing proof that we're doing a good job, we first need to begin where the parable does. No servant starts out with his own talents—God gives them all. If you're able to do anything (whether getting out of bed in the midst of a tough bout with depression or dealing kindly with a parent with dementia or composing a symphony), it's because the Lord allows.

There was one truly faithful servant who is Lord over all. In his time on earth, he didn't impress by the world's standards. Instead of being declared a "man of great success," he was called the "man of sorrows" (Isaiah 53:3). At the end of his year, he didn't tweet the number of his healings, miracles, and disciples like stats to validate his ministry or diligence, because his life and actions belonged to and were blessed by the Father (John 14:31). The crowning achievement of his ministry and biggest advance against the enemy resulted in his death (Hebrews 2:14). In his most important act, he appears at his weakest—bound and bloodied, tied to a tree and condemned. And yet his talents multiplied exponentially as the God of all restored him to his place as king over all things.

If the cross of Christ is the pinnacle of perfect stewardship and faithfulness, then it's possible our perception of achievement and success needs an adjustment. A successful life as a Christian is one where our day's work—no matter how ordinary, small, and unseen—is received joyfully and completed diligently in the strength that God supplies. Today, let all you accomplish be wrapped up in all he accomplished.

⋙ Additional Reading ⋘

> Matthew 25:14-30
>
> Colossians 3:23-24
>
> John 14:15

⋙ Questions for Reflection ⋘

I am weak

- What has God given you to accomplish today, and what resources are you lacking to accomplish it?

- What types of achievements do you tend to feel guilty for not reaching? Where did those expectations come from, and are they biblical?

He is strong

- What were/are Jesus's greatest accomplishments? How do those compare to the world's definition of success?

- How does Jesus Christ's success impact you as you steward the life God has given you?

17

WHEN PEOPLE MAKE YOU FEEL SMALL

*The Son of Man came not to be served but to
serve, and to give his life as a ransom for many.*

MATTHEW 20:28

I arrived early for my spa appointment, trying to play it cool and hide my excitement. An afternoon in a robe and slippers, shuffling between the sauna, a massage appointment, and the container of chocolate-covered almonds, was exactly what I'd hoped for in a day of ultimate relaxation. When the spa technician greeted me and began to show me around, I took mental notes of each little amenity. We were ending the tour in the locker room, where a flurry of women were transitioning from one luxury to the next, when a woman stopped the spa tech with a scowl.

"Tell me how to set my locker again," she barked, though she'd just overheard the tech share the instructions with me.

As the technician calmly started to repeat the directions, the woman held up her hand. "No!" She shifted to a harsher, growling voice. "Actually, I don't really care. This is terrible. Forget it."

An awkward silence hung over the locker room as lotioned faces looked up to see what was going on. All eyes had found the spa technician, who stood there blushing and stunned after the decades-older guest "put her in her place."

Moments like this make me cringe. I've worked in the service industry. I've seated, waited, and bused tables, helped women find and purchase beauty products, worked in homes as a nanny who carried out multiple responsibilities around the house, I've been a teacher serving students, and I've helped tenants at an apartment management company. In all those jobs I've lived the same moment I witnessed the spa technician suffer through— dissatisfied people "putting me in my place" and treating me with unnecessary rudeness. In fact, some people even seemed to enjoy using their wealth, power, and authority as an excuse to demand their way. If you want to know what someone thinks about weakness, watch how they treat people they've paid to serve them.

Are you in a position of serving? Maybe you're employed as a concierge, finding just the right fit for your guests' needs, or you're a nurse caring for the medical and hygiene needs of your patients. Maybe you manage a customer service line, and you deal with hostile questions about billing and damaged products. Or maybe you're a mom who spends much of your day changing diapers, scrubbing stains out of pants, wiping counters, and getting people food. As you serve others, perhaps you've been treated as "less than," you've felt "less than," or you've wondered if your work even matters.[1]

Those of us who struggle with the weakness of serving can find shelter in Jesus. Over and over in the Gospels, Jesus sees and intentionally approaches the positionally weak (the lowly, the servants, and the culturally unimportant) with dignity and care. And though he is Lord, able to demand obedience even from the wind and the waves, he doesn't leverage his power and position for selfish gain. Instead, he gives us the gain, coming to serve in a way that reveals his kingdom and offers citizenship through salvation in his name (Mark 10:25). In Paul's letter to the Philippians, we get a profound description of the mind of Christ when we learn he "did not count equality with God a thing to be grasped, but emptied himself, by taking the form of a servant" (Philippians 2:6-7). Jesus not only understands serving; he chose it.

Being I AM, Jesus could have inhabited any part of society or held unmatched earthly authority (John 8:58). He could have held political power or been an earthly king or high priest. He could have lived in an area of the world or held a profession

---

1. We don't have to be subject to others' abuse of authority, and we should take action to report it and stop others from doing harm. If you are experiencing bullying or abuse in your service job, please reach out to the appropriate superior at work, a trusted friend, or law enforcement.

that brought him social esteem and earthly riches. He could have chosen to influence people through traditional means, getting into the most positionally powerful spot available until all eyes were on him and he had instant credibility. Yet he chose an earthly position of weakness—living in a small village, working as a carpenter, rubbing shoulders with the outcast, and living in the shadows of Jewish society.

As you consider your days and maybe even wrestle with the social embarrassment that can come with positional weakness—as you find yourself in roles that aren't as powerful, impressive, and important as others—will you remember that you ultimately serve Christ (Colossians 3:23-24)? Whatever you do, you do unto him, "for I was hungry and you gave me food, I was thirsty and you gave me drink, I was a stranger and you welcomed me, I was naked and you clothed me, I was sick and you visited me, I was in prison and you came to me. . . . Truly, I say to you, as you did it to one of the least of these my brothers, you did it to me" (Matthew 25:35-40). Serving Christ means walking in his ways, and as you serve Jesus, remember that your "place" is always safe in his kingdom (John 14:2).

Just as Jesus says, "Many who are first will be last, and the last first," we can rest assured that our Lord sees our earthly position and ultimately rewards any service or sacrifice in his name (Matthew 19:29-30). In your everyday work, you can be confident that service is good and glorifies God. Serve with joy because you serve the Lord—who loves, honors, and rewards even the lowliest work done unto him.

⫸ **Additional Reading** ⫷

Matthew 25:31-46

Philippians 2:1-18

Colossians 3:23-24

⫸ **Questions for Reflection** ⫷

I am weak

- In what areas of life do you experience the positional weakness of serving?
- Describe how the world or the culture you're in tends to view service (either broadly or specifically as a job or vocation). How much of this thinking has seeped into your own view of it?

He is strong

- How can you be sure that Jesus values service and doesn't see it as "less than"?
- How does knowing that God "put you in your place" in his kingdom, as his child, change the way you approach your serving today?

18

WHEN YOU CHICKEN OUT

*We are not of those who shrink back and are destroyed,
but of those who have faith and preserve their souls.*

HEBREWS 10:39

Growing up, I lived a short distance from an amusement park called Worlds of Fun. The proximity meant our family could visit at least once each summer, and much more as I got older. When I finally stretched over the height limit, I tested out two full-scale roller coasters: the Orient Express and the Timber Wolf. The first was an early-'80s installment that boasted the first ever "Kamikaze Curve,"[1] and the wooden

---

1. Wikipedia, s.v. "Orient Express (roller coaster)," https://en.wikipedia.org/wiki/Orient_Express_(roller_coaster).

Timber Wolf warned by way of a sign at the entrance that "extreme vibrations and roughness are a nature of this ride. Do not be alarmed."[2]

As I waited in the relentless Kansas City heat for what felt like hours, I often had second thoughts. Before I ever reached the front of the line, my stomach tied itself in knots at the sound of screams and the rumble of cars overhead. But I stayed, inching ahead a few minutes at a time. When it was my turn to be loaded into the car, I'd look off to the side where the orange "chicken exit" sign offered me a snarky way out, and I contemplated my final decision. If fear took over, I knew I could sneak out the side door and avoid the coaster altogether—within minutes, I could be safely down a hidden ramp to the black asphalt below.

Different ideas come to mind when I think of a person who "chickens out." Sometimes I think of someone who was asked to do something foolish and dangerous, but who has the courage and wisdom to walk away. The taunts of "chicken" are the words of a bully. But other times, "chickening out" brings to mind images of someone who is timorous, perpetually afraid, or unable to follow through and face a challenge. When I contemplate the nature of my own weakness in the face of hard things, I often wonder if I'm the latter—a person who perpetually takes the easy way out because I lack faith to face hard things.

Have you ever faced this type of weakness? Wanting to slink out a side door when things get tough? Maybe in your life taking the "chicken exit" looks like avoiding the work of training and discipline in motherhood by regularly zoning out on your phone. Maybe it looks like laughing through conversations with friends or co-workers as they gossip or promote a life philosophy that you know doesn't align with the Bible. Or maybe it's the more subtle omission that took place each time you should have shared gospel truth, offered prayer, given a hug, or spoken Scripture to encourage a friend, but you instead imagined the possible reactions and rejection and decided to keep Christ to yourself.

The Scriptures use a word picture to address the spiritual weakness and fear that can rise in the face of persecution— "shrinking back." In the book of Acts, Paul says that as he preached the gospel, he did *not* shrink back. He recounts his time in Asia and the plots the Jewish leaders concocted to imprison, physically harm, and even kill him. Despite the ploys to stop him, he relates tales of going house to house, teaching in public, and boldly declaring repentance and the need for faith in Jesus Christ (Acts 20:18-21). Two times in his meeting with the elders of the Ephesian church he says that he did not "shrink back" from declaring the whole counsel of God (Acts 20:27). Knowing he would face circumstances much scarier than the "extreme vibrations and roughness" of a coaster ride, he doesn't hold tightly to his likeability, dignity, comfort, or even his life but buckles in by the Spirit for the sake of completing his ministry (Acts 20:24).

The term "shrink back" appears in two other places in the New Testament: once in 1 John 2:28 citing the confidence believers can have when we see Christ face-to-face (abiding in him will allow us to fully and freely come to him when he returns), and again in Hebrews 10:38-39 where the writer of Hebrews calls believers to confidence and endurance in the face of trials and persecution, saying "we are not of those who shrink back and are destroyed, but of those who have faith" and move forward.

At the loading dock of the roller coaster, I would contemplate the warning sign and have an overwhelming instinct to "save myself" and do whatever made me most happy and comfortable at that moment.

Faith in Jesus comes with a warning sign too: *Persecution and suffering up ahead. Do not be alarmed* (2 Timothy 3:12; 1 Peter 4:12). The risk inherent in sharing our faith or simply moving forward in confident obedience to God can send us spiraling into thoughts of saving ourselves and staying comfortable. We cling to the illusion of control over our lives and rehearse the reasons why it's not a big deal to disobey—just this one time. We excuse ourselves out the side door and praise our wisdom in avoiding hardship.

But this is where a faithless type of weakness can hijack our ability to board the ride God has for us. There's no doubt that following Christ is hard. But when we follow him, we "lose our lives" as we strap ourselves into his. We trust that no matter what we face, he's preserving us for eternal life.

As we contemplate the risk of sharing Christ and completing whatever ministry he's given us—whether we risk our heart, our reputation, our energy, or even our very life—let us be those who have bold faith to get on the ride.

⋙ **Additional Reading** ⋘

> Hebrews 10:19-39
>
> 1 Peter 2:12-16
>
> Psalm 27

⋙ **Questions for Reflection** ⋘

I am weak

- In what areas of life have you "chickened out" when it came to speaking boldly about Christ or acting in obedience to God?

- When you want to shrink back from walking in courageous faith, what kinds of things go through your mind? What types of excuses do you use or what things do you tell yourself?

He is strong

- Why can you fully entrust your life (including any suffering or trials that might come) to God? What promises give you assurance that he's good and will be with you?

- What is one thing you could do today when you're tempted to shrink back from opportunities to speak about the gospel and God's Word?

19

WHEN YOU NEED HELP

*The Helper, the Holy Spirit, whom the Father will
send in my name, he will teach you all things and
bring to your remembrance all that I have said to you.*

JOHN 14:26

We sat together in the late spring sun, feeling the breeze through the deck screens. I looked over at my husband and saw him watching a YouTube video with something between a laugh and a smile on his face. The man in the video growled, "No one is coming for you. *No one.*" My husband paused the video and explained that he'd been on a kick of listening to motivational speeches. This is partly because he's a just-work-harder, no-excuses kind of guy and partly because motivational speeches make him laugh. He hit play again, and we listened as the intense voice on the phone continued: "No one is coming to push you. No one is coming to tell you to turn the TV off. No one is coming to tell you to get off the couch and exercise. No one."[1] I got bored very quickly and asked him to turn it off—which likely means I'm the type of person who needs a pep talk.

For the next several days, the "No one is coming for you" line from the speech was our running joke. When a huge dirty diaper needed to be changed, I'd hear my husband say, "No one is coming to get you!" and laugh to himself as he went to get a diaper. When I saw a big mess of golf clubs and Amazon boxes in the garage, I called out, "No one is coming to get you!" and started to tidy up. In whatever situation we faced, this phrase reminded us that life is tough, that we're going to face obstacles, and instead of waiting for someone else to complete a task or for the path to get easier, we should start to tackle the job ourselves.

But aside from the joke, I found this phrase distressing. I regularly feel overwhelmed by all that I'm responsible for: my email inbox, household to-do list, and the people I'm called to serve. The thought of facing it on my own is daunting. When I think of my kids facing a tough situation that they aren't mature enough to handle, it's horrible to imagine them facing

---

1. I tried to find this exact motivational speech, but it's lost in YouTube land. For a similar video, see Mel Robbins, "The Hard Truth About Making Your Dreams Come True," Mel Robbins Live, July 27, 2018, https://www.youtube.com /watch?v=JoQEY2sIMTg.

it alone, believing no one is coming to help. Maybe for some people "tough it out on your own" is a great motivator, but for me, it's another reason to stay stuck.

Do you instinctively gather your own strength when you get overwhelmed? Maybe you get revved up by motivational speeches, and the thought that it's you against the problem makes you pull an invisible sword from your scabbard and get going. Perhaps that's what pushes you to steward your physical health, bear with others through conflict, or stay up late and write the paper. Or maybe you're like me: You already feel like a weakling and hope that help will come and pull you limping across the finish line.

The good news for believers who feel inclined to cower at problems is that we're not alone in our challenges and struggles. Someone has come for you: Jesus sent a Helper. Beginning in John chapter 14, Jesus comforts his anxious disciples. Instead of growling, "No one is coming for you. No one is going to help you spread my message—you'll have to face rejection and pain alone. Get ready to tough it out!" he says, "Let not your hearts be troubled" (John 14:1). Then he reassures, "I will not leave you as orphans; I will come to you," and "Peace I leave with you; my peace I give to you. Not as the world gives do I give to you. Let not your hearts be troubled, neither let them be afraid" (John 14:18, 27). Jesus promises to come again to get them and bring them to be with the Father in heaven (John 14:3). He gives them hope and peace for the future (John 14:28).

Perhaps one of the most profound and surprising promises

Jesus made the disciples is that they will not do the work of kingdom building in their own strength. He would send help (John 14:26). Not the trite type of help I offer across the house to a husband who has a bunch of dishes to tackle: "Yep, I'll be there in a minute, honey!" [*walking very slowly and doing a few random chores along the way*]. No, the help Jesus promises is sure. It's powerful. It's timely, because it's God the Holy Spirit.

God makes sure his people get what they need by sending himself. He's the only one who can do the job he's given us to do. If the Holy Spirit dwells in you as a born-again believer, you'll never face a problem alone. You'll never have to fix it yourself. Someone is coming for you. He already has.

When you need to pray but you're sad and you're not sure what to say, he intercedes on your behalf in just the right way (Romans 8:26-27). When you're out of solutions for a confusing and seemingly impossible situation, he supplies hope (Romans 15:13). When you face temptations head-on, he gives strength to respond like Christ (Galatians 5:16). When you're not sure how to talk about your faith with others or to display God's glory in your life, he works through you in bold and unexpected ways (John 15:26). He knows your thoughts and motivations and gives you the mind of Christ so you can understand the things of God (1 Corinthians 2:10-13). In these ways and more, he is always there to help you live as a Christ follower.

In the face of life's responsibilities and challenges, we don't have to tough it out. We can lean on the One whose strength is never threatened.

⟫ **Additional Reading** ⟪

John 14

Romans 8:26-27

1 Corinthians 2:10-13

⟫ **Questions for Reflection** ⟪

I am weak

- Have you ever been overwhelmed by the thought of facing a challenge or trial alone? Why is that a troubling thought?

- In what areas of life do you need supernatural help and strength?

He is strong

- Dwell on the truth that God is an ever-present help in trouble. Thinking on all you read about the Holy Spirit, how is this true, and what help do you have available right now?

- Write down one way you will ask the Spirit for help where you need it today.

20

WHEN YOU DROP THE BALL

*We have this treasure in jars of clay, to show that the
surpassing power belongs to God and not to us.*

2 CORINTHIANS 4:7

Every once in a while, I feel like I have it all together.
Whether for an afternoon, a few days, or a week, I get
into a groove. I not only remember the appointment but
even make it there on time. I have margin available to make a
wholesome meal for a sick friend. I'm tempted to give in to the
four-year-old begging to have a random piece of candy, but I
don't. I meet my deadlines and give a gracious response to a
hurting friend. I remember to text everyone back. I know I'm
not perfect and have limitations, but this kind of streak feels

like the rush of repeatedly making contact with a tennis ball. The challenge comes my way and I smack it back. *Not today, Satan!* For a time, I have the power to hold it together.

But I've also experienced the subsequent crash of missing the shot and letting the ball drop. Within seconds of my last win, I need to apologize for running late, neglecting to answer texts, and getting buried under emails. I'm forgetful. The stress of life bubbles over into a curt response to my unsuspecting husband's question. I leave the list and the laundry to pile up while I click "next episode." I thought I was holding it together, but my fragility gets the last word.

All the examples listed above are understandable and often have reasonable explanations. We're all human and need to rest. Running late or streaming my favorite TV shows isn't always sin. But the point stands that because we're human, our power and performance are fickle. A lot rides on us having good circumstances and good health. We have the illusion of power when everything is near-perfect—when we feel energized and on our game, it's our favorite season of the year, or others are supportive of us. But eventually one of life's blows—whether mental, physical, spiritual, or relational—creates a crack. We're often one household virus, bad night's sleep, strained back, unwanted diagnosis, lost job, or argument with a spouse away from feeling powerless and out of control.

In his second letter to the Corinthian church, Paul talks about these types of circumstances, and worse—being afflicted, perplexed, and struck down (2 Corinthians 4:8-9). These words give a picture of someone overwhelmed by problems and trials that press in from every side. They show a person who is going without the necessary resources, in a pinch, and feeling uncertain of what to do. We can imagine a person suddenly being humbled by circumstances, laid waste by life, and walking through intense persecution. And while Christians can walk through significant times of struggle, leading to feelings of floundering, fear, and frustration, Paul assures us that our lack doesn't portray the whole truth: We are not without hope. Not completely crushed. Not destined to despair. Not forsaken by the Father. Not utterly destroyed. Our existence can't be distilled down to people who hold it together on some days and let life fall apart on others; we're always fragile vessels holding a treasure (2 Corinthians 4:7).

If I had a treasure, let's say a priceless jewel, I'd keep it somewhere very safe. Maybe in a bank or a vault or someplace remote where it would be hard for someone to find and steal. I'd want to fortify it against every type of threat so I could keep possession of it. I'd never toss the jewel into a bowl on my kitchen counter for "safekeeping." One small hand in search of a snack would send the jewel tumbling out onto the floor! But in some ways, that's exactly what God does. He puts his treasure—his Spirit, his kingdom, his Son—inside of a jar of clay: a human believer. Inside something that can be easily cracked, toppled, and broken. Inside something common and unfortified. Inside something relatively weak. Why would he do that? According to Paul's letter, when we're frazzled and forgotten, confused and hurt, or attacked and struggling, the treasure holds us together and proclaims the surpassing power of God in us.

Going back to the idea of a priceless jewel in a bowl on the counter, what if despite the little hands dipping into the bowl, the mishaps of ordinary life, or the bowl being knocked over, jostled around, and cracked, the jewel always remained unharmed? Wouldn't we call it a miracle? At my house, I would consider a perfectly preserved jewel in a busted kitchen counter bowl a supernatural power at work, because there is no way the bowl could keep it safe from the perils of family life. It must be a jewel like no other.

As jars, we're fickle, fragile vessels, not equipped, strong enough, or smart enough for the treasure we contain. But there's great hope because our weakness serves to emphasize God's power. This is why Paul later says he boasts of his weakness so that the power of Christ can be seen working in and through him all the more (2 Corinthians 12:9).

You might have days where you feel you're single-handedly holding everything together, but this is not a reason to boast. You're a jar of clay. Rejoice and thank God for the smooth circumstances and strength. Resist the temptation of pride— don't chalk it up to your own goodness. On the flipside, don't disdain the days where your cracks start showing. You're a jar of clay. God uses every crack and fissure to show how well he can preserve his treasure in us, provide for us, and execute his perfect and good plans despite our imperfect persons and circumstances. To show that even if we die in these "jars," we will be resurrected. "So we do not lose heart" (2 Corinthians 4:16). It's not up to us to hold all things together; it's up to the Lord (Colossians 1:17).

⋙ *Additional Reading* ⋘

2 Corinthians 4

Matthew 13:44-46

Colossians 1:15-23

⋙ *Questions for Reflection* ⋘

I am weak

- Today, do you feel like you're holding it together, or do you feel like your cracks are showing? In what way?

- How can you relate to Paul's words in 2 Corinthians 4? In what ways have you felt afflicted, perplexed, and struck down in life?

He is strong

- Create a list of the qualities and actions of Christ as listed in Colossians 1:15-23. How does this list give you confidence and assurance in his power and strength?

- When you face hardship today, how will the knowledge of God's power in your weakness change your response?

21

WHEN YOU WANT
TO BE THE BEST

At that time the disciples came to Jesus, saying,
"Who is the greatest in the kingdom of heaven?"

MATTHEW 18:1

Anytime I dole out a compliment in my house, it's only a matter of seconds before I hear, "But what about me, Mom? How am I doing?" No matter how subtle the comment or how clearly deserving the recipient, my other kids' eyes snap up from their Legos, spelling homework, or dishwasher duty with a desperate desire to know they too are doing a great job. Once I reassure them that yes, they are all doing good, someone almost always asks, "But, Mom, who is doing *the best?*"

My children are not the first group of people to desire greatness. Since Cain and Abel, siblings have been sizing each other up in search of approval, wanting to know that before God and others, they are the most favored (Genesis 4:1-10). And today, while most of us don't think we burn with murderous anger or grumble with the Lord about the worthiness of our sacrifices, we still find ways to measure our greatness, and we seethe with envy when we fall short.

Maybe you have a friend with a wildly successful online business or who accumulates likes and comments when they post well-formulated thoughts on social media. Maybe you have a sister or brother who seems to be "Mom and Dad's favorite," with a special college degree, an impressive career, or the honor of being first to bring grandchildren into the family. Maybe you have co-workers whose names are always dropped alongside praise in meetings, who never seem to be stressed or harried as they climb the corporate ladder. Regardless of the circumstances, when we see others achieving greatness or being recognized for it, we can burn inside.

I'm familiar with the longing for validation and the seething that happens when it doesn't come. I'm still caught off guard when I have to wrestle with the self-loathing that accompanies going without praise. I'm familiar with being like the child who hears, "Yes, I see you're trying, but little Rachel is doing an *especially* good job." I've not always been invited to the cool table, nominated for the special award, or picked for the lead role. When I've seen my weakness or silliness and sensed that whatever I offered wasn't enough, I've felt my face grow hot and my cheeks flush as my insides tense and turn.

Have you ever stopped to wonder what this burning is all about? Why do we care so much about being seen, validated, and praised before others? Why do we care so much about greatness?

Because we were created for our great God. Deep down, we want to know we're seen, loved, cherished, and chosen by someone great. The Bible tells us that God's "greatness is unsearchable" and his "is the greatness and the power and the glory and the victory and the majesty" (Psalm 145:3; 1 Chronicles 29:11). When we long for greatness, we're longing for God. But when we long to *be* the greatest, we're longing to *be* God. See how easily those two things can get confused?

Perhaps this is why Jesus rebukes his disciples when they ask, "Who is the greatest in the kingdom of heaven?" and when James and John ask what they have to do to get the best spot at Jesus's right hand (Matthew 18:1; Mark 10:35). In both cases, Jesus gives a worldview-shattering response. Where the disciples aspire for greatness and glory through Jesus's stamp of approval and a prominent place by the person in power, Jesus shows them that true greatness isn't attainable for the proud and power hungry. Greatness is found in humility. The greatest person is the one who serves (Matthew 18:4; Mark 10:43). Additionally, Jesus points out that the disciples don't really know what they are seeking—it's God who distributes our gifts and position, and Jesus (the truly great one) is going to die as a ransom for many.

In this, Jesus shows that greatness is not having the biggest following of all our friends online, getting invited to the corporate inner circle, being given compliments and awards, or visibly succeeding at all we put our hands to. It's not being publicly lauded and complimented as the best mom, homemaker, volunteer, or prayer warrior. Our greatest moments are the ones where we point to the Great One.

This is good news for those of us who fall short of the world's brand of greatness, because true greatness is still available as we know and serve Christ. To fill our desire for great things, we can fill our hearts and lives with the unsearchable greatness of God: We can read his Word, marvel at his creation, and rejoice with his people. And to be great in the kingdom of heaven, we can accept our weaknesses and limitations while taking hold of our talents and resources—true greatness lies in glorifying our great God in all we do, every day.

Additional Reading

Matthew 18:1-4

Mark 10:38-45

Psalm 145

➤➤ *Questions for Reflection* ◀◀

I am weak

- In what areas of life do you long to hear that you are great or are doing a great job? Who do you want to hear that from, and how would that affirmation help?

- How would you define being "great" and how does that contrast with Jesus's definition of greatness?

He is strong

- What attributes of God make him great? How do you see this greatness displayed in creation or in his work in your life?

- What makes Jesus great, and what did that look like in the context of "being a ransom for many"?

—— **22** ——

WHEN YOU'RE UNDER
THE INFLUENCE

*Among them are those who creep into households
and capture weak women, burdened with sins and
led astray by various passions, always learning and
never able to arrive at a knowledge of the truth.*

2 TIMOTHY 3:6-7

Have you ever heard of the Seven Times Factor? Sometimes known as the marketing rule of seven, it's a theory from the 1930s about how many times a potential customer has to hear or see a product before they make a purchase. In the modern age of social media, brands and influencers alike are demolishing the goal of seven—in some cases getting you to watch upwards of seven videos, images, and posts per day, adding up to hundreds and thousands of exposures over the years.[1] Based on my own experience on social media, I'd say the strategy works.

There was the time I wanted some new workout clothing, and instead of going to the usual places, I purchased from a little-known store online (for quadruple the price). Later, it occurred to me that I never knew this brand existed until someone I follow on Instagram became a brand ambassador and told me about it over and over again. Then there was the time I bought and waited six months for a stone lamp because I'd seen it not just on one designer's Instagram but across multiple accounts over the course of a year. The first time I saw the leggings and the lamp, I scrolled right by (not even registering what I'd seen), but the tenth? The twentieth? The fiftieth? Familiarity and curiosity got the better of me.

Familiarity and influence can be used for good. Sometimes we find a truly helpful product we didn't know we needed, or we discover a good Bible study or Christ-exalting resource. And as was the case for me with the leggings and table decor, you are free to make those purchases, and you won't necessarily regret them. But it's critical to see a bigger connection—to realize that if this kind of influence can happen with objects, it can happen with ideologies. And when these deviate from the Bible, we might not know the cost until it's too late.

Being easily persuaded is the type of weakness that Paul warns about in his second letter to Timothy when he prepares

---

1. "Rule of 8: How Social Media Crushes Old-School Marketing," Digital Dealer, November 29, 2016, https://digitaldealer.com/latest-news/rule-7-social-media-crushes-old-school-marketing/.

readers for the danger of the last days. He mentions over nineteen different categories of sin that will be rampant in this time, including things like ingratitude, materialism, and abuse. In chapter 3, verse 5, he pauses to simply say, "Avoid such people."

Most of us read a text like this and heave a small sigh of relief. It seems feasible to just stay away from obviously "bad" people. But then Paul's warnings get uncomfortable, at least for my modern ears. He says that these evil people will go on the offensive and target women. *Yikes! I don't want to make myself an obvious mark.*

The word "weak" in this passage isn't referring to an inherent moral weakness in women, a lack of physical strength, or a universal gullibility of one gender. It's talking about women who have made themselves foolish, undiscerning, and spiritually flimsy. Specifically, Paul qualifies that these women are "burdened with sins and led astray by various passions, always learning and never able to arrive at a knowledge of the truth" (2 Timothy 3:6-7). The picture here is of women who are looking for something, anything, that may supplement or supersede the care of Christ.

I don't know exactly what behaviors might have characterized a woman in ancient Ephesus who was burdened with sin, led astray by her passions, or never able to arrive at the truth. But I know the possibilities that show up in our lives today: to make it a habit to finish the bottle of wine, to read a pornographic novel, to share salacious stories with our friends, or to be women who pursue any dream or goal we desire without any concern for how it might impact others. Paul speaks to women who are experts in research—constantly searching, clicking, scrolling, listening, and gathering any and every opinion we can without submitting our own to the Word of God. In one way or another, these tendencies can show we don't trust that Christ stands ready and willing to steady our wandering minds, calm our anxious hearts, renew our desires, and restore our lost souls. Women who choose these things display weakness, and not in a good way—they are vulnerable to being snatched by "wolves" (Matthew 7:15; Romans 16:17-18).[2]

Let's circle back to the rule of seven, because the danger of this type of weakness hits closer to home than many of us realize. In today's culture, where are people touting false and godless ideologies (even while disguising themselves as truthful and godly) and coming "into homes" to influence women who are burdened with sin and always looking for a new thing to subscribe to? *Ahem.* You guessed it: social media.

I'm not saying that social media is evil, that influencers are all bad and trying to trick you, or that Instagram and TikTok need to be deleted from your phone. Many women can use social media for good, beautiful, and practical things. But I am saying that as we explore the concept of weakness in Scripture, we have to acknowledge we must fortify ourselves against a certain type of weakness—the kind that comes when God and his Word don't dwell in us richly. How can you be a woman who makes a habit of trusting and looking to Christ?

It starts by acknowledging your own propensity to be

---

2. In other passages, men in particular and all Christians in general are warned of something similar. All Christians need to be on guard against wolves.

subtly led astray over a long period of time and then taking this risk to the Good Shepherd, who protects his sheep from wolves. Practically, this looks like studying Scripture, solidifying yourself in a healthy church and gospel community where you meet together regularly, having good Christian friends who aren't afraid to ask hard questions or speak truth, and regularly evaluating what entertainment and influences you listen to. When your compass starts to seem a little off—when you feel yourself getting bitter, burdened, disillusioned, and tempted to turn to something or someone other than God—know the warning signs and turn back to Christ, the only influencer who most certainly leads to life.

⋙ Additional Reading ⋘

2 Timothy 3:1-9

Romans 16:17-20

John 10:11-15

Questions for Reflection

I am weak

- Can you think of a recent time when you were subtly and unknowingly influenced to think or buy something? Explain how you went from "first exposure" to your final thoughts, actions, or purchases. What do you observe about that process?

- What, if any, qualities of weakness that Paul describes in 2 Timothy 3:6-7 do you see in your own life?

He is strong

- What things has God provided to fortify you from being undiscerning and spiritually flimsy? Which of those things do you engage in regularly, and which things would you like to do more of?

- How does knowing that Jesus is the Good Shepherd change your desire to be with him, listen to him, and stay close to him?

23

WHEN YOU THINK IT'S UP TO YOU

God will ransom my soul from the power
of Sheol, for he will receive me.

PSALM 49:15

It's funny and frustrating to watch a determined four-year-old work to move something more than half their weight. At some point or another, while going through an "I do it *myself*, Mommy" phase, each of our children has tried to hold something that's too heavy for them. I can picture their little determined faces, lips pursed and teeth clenched, cheeks red, forehead and neck veins bulging, trying with all their might to lift the family library tote or Daddy's work bag. I've even seen a preschooler get frustrated and try to move our living room couch—kicking it in anger when it won't yield. As a parent, it's hard not to laugh. After all, the strength of a four-year-old isn't very strong at all. I try to hide my grin as I gently ask, "Would you like some help?"

It would be nice to say this is unique to my children, but I also overestimate my strength. There was the time I tried to rearrange the ten-foot couches in our living room—I technically got them moved, but there's a scratch across our hardwood floor to prove I shouldn't have tried. Aside from my muscles, I've tried to overcome grief with the strength of a stoic, temptation with the power of my flesh, and relational conflict with the fire of my words. Whether through more time, money, research, conversation, brainstorming, or networking, I've worn myself out trying to hold the weight of things too big for me to carry.

In our modern world, with access to deep wells of information on the internet, millions of self-help gurus, home gyms, financial credit, and the opportunity for press coverage, we can all start to overestimate our strength. Maybe like me, you're tempted to think you're one full-body transformation, supplement regimen, master class, new business, cross-country move, makeover, house refresh, career change, or closet organization away from total life domination. You face life's troubles with a penchant for hard work, a clenched jaw, and declare, "I'll do it myself. Just watch."

But you know as well as I do that when it comes to life, though we're able to make temporal and surface-level changes—even affecting our external appearance or circumstances—life ultimately won't yield. Trying to impose our will and muscle through is like straining to push over a mountain.

In Psalm 49, the choirmaster poetically considers what makes someone strong in the face of life's troubles. Is it a big checking account balance and access to resources? A wide personal network, healthy boundaries, and thriving relationships? Being the smartest person in the room? Having influence over what others think and do? Is it enough to have confidence and believe we can? Do social media bio titles and office-framed achievements help? In short, no. The choirmaster shows that though we might do well for ourselves and initially look blessed, or though we might appear strong as we accumulate wisdom, wealth, and notoriety, ultimately every person is headed toward the grave.

Like the frustrated four-year-olds who can't carry all their toys at one time, we find that our strength is actually not very strong at all. That when we die, we "will carry nothing away" and "glory will not go down after [us]" (Psalm 49:16-17). No matter how much temporary "strength" we accumulate in this life, whether physical, financial, social, or mental, it is not enough to keep us from death. We are dust trying to hold rocks.

In times of trouble, both now and on judgment day, we have access to strength that stands firm and defeats death in Christ. And as the choirmaster says, "God will ransom my soul. . . . He will receive me" (Psalm 49:15). We can face trouble and say, "Whom shall I fear?" when we are on the side of the One with ultimate and eternal strength. Not even the sacrifice of our very lives is enough to save ourselves or another person when it counts. Only God can ransom through the sacrifice of Christ. Only his blood is strong enough to save (Psalm 49:15).

In the meantime, we can accept our relative weakness and turn to God for help and strength. When I've seen a preschooler groan with frustration, unable to move something heavy, I have the perspective that it shouldn't be a big deal to ask for help with something I was never meant to carry. And just as I stood ready to help the four-year-old who would take a deep breath, stop kicking the library bag, and humbly ask me to carry it, our heavenly Father wants to put his power and glory on display as he carries us through heavy experiences in life. He wants to bear our burdens and welcomes our worries (Psalm 68:19; 1 Peter 5:7). We must only admit our weakness to receive his strength.

⫸ Additional Reading ⫷

> Psalm 49
> 1 Corinthians 1:26-31
> 2 Corinthians 12:10

⫸ *Questions for Reflection* ⫷

I am weak

- Can you think of a time when you saw someone try to lift or carry something that was obviously too heavy for them? What do you learn about relative strength and what God has given you to carry?

- In what area of life are you tempted to muscle through and handle heavy things by your own strength? What does this look like? How do you feel and respond when your efforts don't produce the result you desired?

He is strong

- From Psalm 49, write a list of the qualities, achievements, and areas of life that people try to use to obtain strength. What does this psalm say is the ultimate result or benefit of having these things?

- In the face of all types of strength that the world values, who ultimately has the power to save and uphold in times of trouble? How do you know?

24

WHEN YOU PUT YOURSELF OUT THERE

We have spoken freely to you,
Corinthians; our heart is wide open.

2 CORINTHIANS 6:11

Sometimes I look back on an evening with friends, a meeting with a new co-worker, a discussion in Bible study, or a birthday party with other parents and cringe. Instead of being a fly on the wall, I put myself out there, jumping full steam into the conversation. I asked questions and gave ideas. I told personal stories and listened to the stories of others. I looked for opportunities to forge relationships. Maybe I even shared something vulnerable or pressed into a friend's hurt or concern.

But later, in the car ride home, in the silence of a walk, or with my head on my pillow—I start to replay the conversations. *Did I talk too much? I should have just sat there. I probably sounded so weird and annoying. Did I misspeak or offend someone? Are they analyzing what I said?* I worry that I put too much of myself out there—that I was too much.

For me, conversation replay is often about my discomfort with vulnerability. When I stay on the quiet fringes of the conversation with my thoughts held tightly to my chest, I might not get to know anyone better or move things along, but at least I feel safe. If I don't share much, I can't be rejected for it. If I'm not known, I can't look silly. Sometimes putting myself out there is exactly what it sounds like—being exposed and unprotected against verbal or relational backlash. While there *are* times people overshare, giving information that wasn't theirs to give or being inappropriately intimate or graphic as they tell stories, this is different from wrestling with feelings of vulnerability in the path to being known.

Especially as ambassadors of Christ's love and good news, we need to recognize that knowing and being known is part of the job—something Paul and Timothy were familiar with. As they traveled and shepherded churches, listening to hurts and sharing their hearts, giving wisdom and guiding people in the way of Christ, Paul described their posture: hearts wide open (2 Corinthians 6:11). Their willingness to love and be vulnerable was an asset.

Paul and Timothy knew the insufficiency of their words and instructions apart from God (2 Corinthians 3:5). But they also knew they could be bold because of their future hope. Someday, regardless of how people received them on earth, they would be with Christ, fully transformed into his image (2 Corinthians 3:18, 4:17). They could have courage and not lose heart, because they feared the opinion of God more than the opinion of man (2 Corinthians 3:12, 5:11). This ministry, which included open hearts as they shared and lived the gospel, wasn't about them; it was about Christ.

Because the goal was that Christ be known and his kingdom expanded, no act of slander, no rejection, no misunderstanding or misconstruing of their message, no misspeak could cause them to abandon their work, close off, or quit, even though they knew the risks. Their security in Christ was greater. They knew that in the midst of any exposure they felt, any vulnerability they experienced, in an ultimate way, they were known, seen, accepted, loved, and kept by Christ. They could speak out in the world because he had called them into his kingdom.

When you replay conversations and feel vulnerable, you can feel certain your words were not perfect. Maybe you did jump in a little too quickly or add in a few unnecessary details. That's human. (They probably did too. You might not have even noticed!) But don't count it as a big mistake to share from the heart and listen to others. Your willingness to go first, to open up, share, and ask questions might be just the thing God uses to prompt deeper conversations.

In this feeling of weakness, remember the true depth of vulnerability every person will experience before the throne of God when every thought and intention of the heart and every deed is not only exposed but judged. All of us are fully known today. There is no part of you that's hidden from God.

You can't overshare with him, because he knows more about you than you do. Through Christ, you are not only known but welcome (Romans 15:7). There is no detail about you that isn't seen, forgiven, and redeemed. Living known and accepted by God gives you freedom to be vulnerable and welcome others into Christ-honoring fellowship.[1]

Tim Keller puts it this way in his short book *The Freedom of Self-Forgetfulness*:

> You see, the verdict is in. And now I perform on the basis of the verdict. Because He loves me and He accepts me, I do not have to do things just to build up my résumé. I do not have to do things to make me look good. I can do things for the joy of doing them. I can help people to help people— not so I can feel better about myself, not so I can fill up the emptiness.[2]

We can speak and share, growing in relationship with others from a posture of full acceptance, and we can do it with humility and joy. Take your next conversation replay to the Lord in humility, asking him to help. If you said something

---

1. I want to note here that even though vulnerability is an important part of growing in relationships and ministering to others, it must be practiced with wisdom. There are some people with whom it's not wise to share. We need to have self-control and boundaries. We shouldn't endlessly open ourselves up to those who are cruel, foolish, bullying, or abusive. The aim of this devotion is simply to give courage in the midst of the feeling of vulnerability that accompanies regular sharing in healthy relationships. If you aren't sure what this wisdom looks like in your own life or you have a question about a specific relationship, please reach out to a trusted friend, mentor, pastor, or counselor.

2. Timothy Keller, *The Freedom of Self-Forgetfulness* (Chorley, UK: 10Publishing, 2012), 40.

you truly shouldn't have, repent and apologize. Otherwise, move forward with courage and continue sharing with wisdom and a wide-open heart.

Additional Reading

> 2 Corinthians 5:21
>
> Psalm 139
>
> Ephesians 4:29

Questions for Reflection

I am weak

- Can you think of a recent time when you replayed a conversation and felt embarrassed about what you said? Was this because you actually said something wrong or because you felt vulnerable to rejection as you were getting to know someone?

- What are you worried people will think of you as you open up and humbly share about yourself in conversation?

He is strong

- After reading Psalm 139, what comfort do you have in realizing you are fully and deeply known by God? Why can you trust God with your heart and life, even as you are exposed before him?

- How does knowing you'll never be rejected by God through Christ give you courage as you get to know others and do ministry?

=== 25 ===

WHEN YOU THINK
YOU GOT THIS

When he was strong, he grew proud, to his destruction.

2 CHRONICLES 26:16

When I first started writing publicly, every little thing felt like a huge win. I was greener than fresh-cut spring grass and didn't personally know one published author or professional editor. For years I wrote in obscurity during naptime and worked up the courage to publish entries to my blog. I remember the feeling of excitement the first time someone (other than a friend or family member) reshared one of my posts, the honor of being asked to collaborate with another blogger, and the thrill of seeing my first byline on a ministry website. I wrote in full awareness of my weakness. I viewed every opportunity as an undeserved gift from God.

But as time passed, the readers and bylines grew more numerous. I became an editor myself and even secured a book deal. Though I still knew everything was a gift, I was tempted to forget it. They say familiarity breeds contempt, and I was starting to get comfortable. The fresh, green girl in me started to feel more like a well-established tree, and it became too easy to mistake my success as my own doing. I see how quickly someone can grow proud, and it makes me grateful for every way that God allows me to feel weak.

If there is a king in Scripture (apart from Jesus) who had a weak and humble beginning, it's probably King Uzziah. Taking over his father's throne as a teenage boy, he was in no position to lead a struggling nation. Overwhelmed and maybe even panicked, Uzziah decided to follow the Lord and rely on him for the strength to lead. I imagine that he lived aware he was greener than a fresh-sprouted fig, that a keen sense of his own inability propelled him to seek God so diligently, along with wise counsel from others. His weakness kept him tightly tethered to the Lord.

As time went on, the Lord blessed and strengthened King Uzziah. He grew into a man who commanded a strong, victorious, and innovative military. His rule was so successful, his kingdom so secure, that his fame spread to the surrounding nations. But no longer a desperate teenager with no hope or resources, he began to take his strength for granted. His assumed success led to pride, and pride to destruction.

Before we pick on King Uzziah, let's pause and look at our own hearts. When we have all we need—when things are going well and we feel strong and successful—how often do we stop turning to the Lord, stop recognizing his hand in our life? Aren't we guilty of thinking that our life works so well because we work so hard? Or that the abundance of our resources or the strength of our lives is owing to our own abilities, stewardship, grit, and savvy? Aren't we quick to forget that the sun and rain that nourished our roots and expanded our branches came to us as a gift from the Lord? How faded are our memories of our humble beginnings, of our early days of need, and of the things that were given to us?

Perhaps it's just the passing of time that clouds your weakness, making it hard to see why you're still in desperate need of God's help—or perhaps it's something more. A confidence, disdain, and hatred of your own weakness. You don't look back on your beginnings as a sweet season of reliance on the Lord but as a season you never want to walk in again. You prefer feeling able and in control as you seemingly chart your own destiny. While the world might call this strength, Scripture shows us the backward reality of God's kingdom—with God, we are strong; apart from him, we are weak.

King Uzziah gets the definition of strength wrong as his pride emboldens him to defy God's laws by burning incense in the temple. God strikes him with leprosy. As King Uzziah is cut off from his people and set apart as unclean, we see a picture of pride as a leprosy of the soul, cutting us off from the Lord.

With each victory, Uzziah could have stripped himself of

his pride and humbled himself before God, the giver of all good gifts, but he didn't. And ultimately, when confronted for his arrogance before the Lord, he refused the chance to repent. Uzziah's pride was the final note of his life, but our pride doesn't have to be the final note of ours. Perhaps we don't need to rewind to our humble beginnings, but we do need a fresh taste of humility. To remember that regardless of how smart, efficient, driven, disciplined, determined, successful, wealthy, or famous we are, this does not make us right before a holy God, nor does it entitle us to our gifts.

Jesus came from humble beginnings in Bethlehem, but he never fell from grace. He was royal, gifted, famous, and successful in every act of ministry he put his hand to, yet he was never corrupted by pride. At every stage of his ministry, we see Jesus turning to the Father in prayer and praise and acknowledgment. Jesus's life, death, and resurrection show us a picture of success and humility—perfect strength who came to serve. If Jesus Christ is not too important and independent to go without intimate dependence on the Father, then neither are we exempt from a posture of dependence on the Lord. Perhaps we have a lot to learn from humble beginnings, most importantly how much we truly need the Lord.

⋙ **Additional Reading** ⋘

2 Chronicles 6:1-23

Proverbs 11:2

John 15:5

⋙ **Questions for Reflection** ⋘

I am weak

- Reflect on your "early days" in an aspect of your life. What made you feel weak when you were just starting out?

- In what areas of life are you tempted to "assume your success" instead of depending on God for provision and help?

He is strong

- Spend a few minutes creating a list of the good things God has given you and then answer the question "Did you do anything special to deserve all of these things, or are they a gift of his grace?" Why or how do you know?

- What would it look like to acknowledge your need for God and depend on him today? (List at least two specific actions.)

26

WHEN YOU'RE BETTER TOGETHER

*Let us consider how we may spur one another
on toward love and good deeds, not giving up
meeting together, as some are in the habit of
doing, but encouraging one another—and all
the more as you see the Day approaching.*

HEBREWS 10:24-25 NIV

In the warmer months, I bike out of my driveway onto the open road and pedal my way to a nearby trail. I love to cycle beside the cornfields, watching them go from tilled black soil in early spring to brown, ready-to-harvest stalks in October. The butterflies, the ditch flowers, the smell of laundry in the nearby town, and the neighbors that wave while I ride make it comfortable and picturesque. Knowing my love for cycling, I thought I'd enjoy a Peloton. *Pretty much the same thing, right?*

I clicked in my shoes alongside my husband for a side-by-side test ride at his brother's house. My sister-in-law got me water and a towel—which I was pretty sure I didn't need because I don't sweat that much on my own bike—and we were off. The instructor was upbeat and talkative, the music pumping through the speakers. We could both see a leaderboard on the screen with hundreds of people taking the class at the same time, making it easy to track progress. I could even see my sister-in-law's output record and how I was matching up to it second by second.

Thirty minutes later, I unclicked, panting and drenched with sweat. Aside from pedaling, that was nothing like riding my bike outside! Even though it was harder, I had to admit it was a better workout—I got off the bike feeling a good kind of exhaustion.

Later, I tried to re-create the workout on my own bike. I carefully monitored my speed and heart rate on my watch, trying to match my performance on the Peloton. I told myself to increase my cadence, I listened to motivating music, and I attempted to ride as hard as I could. But after thirty minutes, I came nowhere close to the level of output I had clipped into the guided stationary ride. Alone, I couldn't perform with the same strength and endurance as I could with others around me, pushing me to do my best.

When it comes to performance, there's power in groups. That's why fitness classes exist at the gym, why Peloton displays stats from other riders on the screen, and why popular advice says that if you're going to start a regular habit of walking, you should go with a friend. It's a phenomenon called social facilitation.[1]

When it comes to feeling weak in an area of life, could it be that you're trying to go it alone? Maybe you want to start a habit of Bible reading and prayer, but it's hard to stay motivated and be consistent. Maybe this isn't limited to Bible reading, and you've been doing the Christian life alone—you had reason to take a break from church, or life circumstances forced one, and now you've been following God, worshipping him, and living your faith for years without the leadership, fellowship, accountability, and discipleship of a local church. Maybe you've been trying to process through doubt and suffering without letting other believers listen and pray.

In Hebrews chapter 10, we don't see a picture of an individual Christian considering how to pursue godliness alone. We see a picture of the way Christians need one another to walk in faith. The NIV translation spotlights our healthy and necessary dependence on one another with the word "spur." When I hear the word "spur," my mind replays a video of a cowboy jutting his spurs into the side of his horse to increase its urgency, speed, and performance. When used correctly, spurs are meant to apply pressure but not pain. This is what the Peloton instructor did to me when he said, "Okay, we're going to increase the cadence and resistance for sixty seconds. You

---

1. Arlin Cuncic, "What Is Social Facilitation?" Verywell Mind, August 27, 2021, https://www.verywellmind.com/an-overview-of-socialfacilitation-4800890.

can do it!" I was uncomfortable, but not injured. He skillfully provoked me to do more than I wanted to. This is why we need other Christians alongside us in life—because through their example, presence, thoughtful questions, well-timed exhortations, and godly actions they prompt us to follow the Lord in a more determined and bold way than we would have on our own.

This concept is paired with another idea in these verses—meeting together regularly with other believers. One of the clearest ways for us to be faithful to this command in our modern day is to meet with other believers regularly by participating in corporate worship at a church. In some circumstances, people are physically unable to meet corporately with other believers on a regular basis as they age, experience significant health challenges, or face the effects of disability. Though we're blessed by one-off meetings with a believing friend and technology that allows us to watch church online, for most of us, they're not a long-term replacement for the norm of meeting together. God breathes new strength into a Christian's heart as we hear voices of other believers praising God, take communion, pray together, and sit under preaching. I can't count the number of times I've felt weak and discouraged, and the act of participating in corporate worship at my local church was the very thing that humbled and encouraged me to keep trusting Christ.

Speaking of encouragement, this is another reason why we need other believers. It's like having fellow soldiers come alongside to provide strength and support, and to say, "Keep going! Let's keep fighting!" It's my husband turning to me during the Peloton ride and saying, "You're doing great! Keep riding!" It's the thing I can't seem to tell myself when I'm alone on a bike trail. Other believers can point out the areas where we're thriving when we feel like we're doing a terrible job, and they can help us see areas of improvement and opportunity when we're not sure what to do.

As you feel weak in the Christian life—whether in your spiritual disciplines, your faith and belief in God's Word, or your motivation to keep growing—as you feel weak in your service to others and your witness in your personal mission field, be strengthened alongside other believers by the power of the Spirit working in the church.

⫸ Additional Reading ⫷

Hebrews 10:19-35

Colossians 3:16

Ephesians 4:1-15

≫ *Questions for Reflection* ≪

I am weak

- Describe a time when being with a partner or in a group setting enhanced your performance, determination, or hard work. Why was this so helpful?

- What is one area of the Christian life where you struggle to make progress or you feel particularly weak and weary?

He is strong

- How has God provided a means of strength in and through the church? How would being with other believers in corporate worship and linking arms for encouragement in specific areas be helpful?

- What is it that really provides the body of Christ with strength and hope, causing the church to endure trials, persecution, and hardship? Is it the strength of the people?

27

WHEN YOU'RE
AT CAPACITY

*Moses said to God, "Who am I that I should go to
Pharaoh and bring the children of Israel out of Egypt?"*

EXODUS 3:11

My husband has always wanted to be a pilot. He's fascinated by airplanes and jumps at any opportunity to ride in one—or for his wife to do so—and that's how I ended up taking a small four-seat Cessna with a family friend across the state line for a writing retreat. I was excited but also a little terrified, which felt justified since the night before I left I had to text the pilot my exact weight, along with the weight of my suitcase. Three people were flying, and with fuel, passengers, and luggage, it was possible to exceed the small plane's capacity. In that case, it would have been difficult to take off, climb, or reach the right altitude. The proper weight, balance, and center of gravity were crucial to having a safe and successful flight. The thought of a small prop plane struggling to take off made removing that second pair of shoes from my bag an easy decision.

Capacity is much simpler to measure for an airplane than to measure in life. Physically, each person has a limit of how much weight they can lift—I can muscle six grocery bags into the house at a time, but I can't hold twelve. Mentally, emotionally, and spiritually, we're much the same, though it's abstract and harder to grasp. Dozens or maybe even hundreds of factors influence our capacity. How much sleep are you getting? Is there unresolved trauma or abuse in your past? What pressures are you facing at home or at work? Did you just receive bad news, or are you grieving a significant loss? Personality, drive, how we've been raised or discipled, or our talents and skills can all impact capacity as well. But regardless of the factors, at some point our hearts can still become like an overweight propeller plane—lagging and struggling, too weak to fly.

There's a common saying in some Christian spaces that addresses our personal capacity: "God would never give you more than you could handle." Is that true? Does God know the capacity of your heart, carefully adding or removing things so as not to overload you? Or does God aim to stretch and grow your capacity, similar to the physical concept of progressive overload, where muscle is built as you gradually push just past the brink of fatigue? Or does God not consider your capacity, intentionally giving you more than you could possibly carry so that his glory will shine through? Aside from the quote (which is definitely not in the Bible), I think it's all of the above.

Let's take, for example, the story of God calling Moses to free Israel from Egypt. God asked Moses to do something impossible—free an entire group of people from slavery, evacuate them from Egypt, and guide them on a difficult journey to the promised land. I can't even begin to capture how much of an overwhelming and unfathomable task this would be for a trained extraction team, let alone one man. God asked Moses to do something beyond what he could handle, even in the best-case scenario. The limited capacity of one person helps explain why Moses pushed back on God's call, first saying, "Who am I?" and then progressing to "They will not believe me or listen to my voice," and "Oh, my Lord, I am not eloquent," and "Oh, my Lord, please send someone else" (Exodus 3:11; 4:1, 10, 13). But God knew about Moses's capacity level and explained to Moses that it was impossible for *him* but not for God. *God* would be the one to do it (3:7-12).

When Moses considered this task, he turned his attention to his own capacity and fixated on his limits. He stoked God's anger when he emphasized his own inabilities instead of marveling at God's immense abilities. Since Moses couldn't fathom God's strength filling in his own weakness, God reassured Moses, providing support that he could wrap his mind around—God gave Moses the script by telling him exactly what he needed to say to his people and to Pharaoh (3:14-15), he gave him a staff that would play a part in the forthcoming miracles (4:1-5), and he gave Moses a partner to help him where his speech and leadership might be lacking (4:14-16). The Lord called Moses, and then he equipped and compelled him to respond in trust. Though God asked Moses to do something beyond his capacity, he didn't leave Moses without his presence and supernatural help. In fact, God was never relying on Moses's capacity level; he was inviting Moses to partner with him in his work to free his people. Similarly, God promises to be the endless well of strength we need, especially when it seems we've been bested by our situation.

God asks his children to do hard and often impossible things, sometimes allowing them to go through intense pain, loss, or persecution, knowing the limits of the frame he created for us (Psalm 103:14). That's another way of saying he is more intimately aware of our humanity than we are. He knows who we are, what we've been through, and what we can handle. Even if we are doubting or hurting, his aim is not to snuff out or break our faith but to strengthen us when we feel vulnerable and broken (Isaiah 42:1,3). When we're at or over our capacity, God wants us to come to Christ with our burdens, letting him carry them so that we might utilize his strength and be given rest in place of burdens (Matthew 11:30). When we're in a tough spot and feel we can't handle another temptation, God promises that he will not tempt us beyond what we can bear, and he will provide a way of escape (1 Corinthians 10:13). And though God might allow us to struggle deeply, he protects us from being driven to total despair or having our true faith destroyed (2 Corinthians 4:8-9).

These are important promises to recall in my day-to-day life as I often feel weak, operating at or over my capacity and wondering why God has given me more than I can handle. I come up against my limits on every side, feeling discouraged because one day I can keep the house clean, make food for everyone, and get to appointments on time, but then the next day I drop the ball on responding to my friend's texts, discipling my kids through a conflict, or practicing therapies with my son. On another day, I try to focus on the balls I dropped only to find a whole other area of life I can't manage. It's like I told my husband before I left for a trip, as he laid out the plans for managing the kids each day: "Of those five things, pick two that you want to do well. You won't be able to do them all!"

I don't have a great answer for the question of why, but I do know it's okay that you have a limited capacity, and I know that in general we should apply wisdom and seek to humbly operate within the bounds of our human limitations. I'm not sure it serves anyone when we pridefully and knowingly attempt to fly beyond our weight rating. But on the other hand, I know God brings trials, circumstances, and kingdom assignments into our lives that are beyond what we can carry—and in those situations, he gets all the glory because there's no other explanation for our ability to fly. Even when we feel too weak, God's strength is ready to carry us through whatever he's called us to do.

⫸ **Additional Reading** ⫷

> Exodus 3-4
>
> Psalm 103
>
> Isaiah 41:10; 43:2

⫸ **Questions for Reflection** ⫷

I am weak

- How would you describe your capacity in life? Do you feel like you are able to handle a lot or a little? What factors tend to impact your personal capacity?

- Think of a time when you felt you were having to operate over your personal capacity. Why was that? Was it self-imposed overload, God-given, or both? How did you respond to those extra burdens in life?

He is strong

- When you feel weak because you're carrying more than you can handle, what might it look like to go to God, asking for help, wisdom, and discernment? How could you involve others to determine where you need to rely on his supernatural strength or where you've pridefully overextended yourself?

- What biblical promises give you the most hope as you face things that feel impossible?

28

WHEN YOU DON'T SEE THE POINT

*Every branch in me that does not bear fruit he
takes away, and every branch that does bear
fruit he prunes, that it may bear more fruit.*

JOHN 15:2

I regret to say that growing up, I was completely disinterested
in my grandma's prolific gardening skills and my mom's
gifts with a strawberry patch. I grew up near a big city, and I
was more eager to try out fine dining than to plant vegetables.
But in my thirties, I finally saw the appeal of spending undue
amounts of time in my yard, bent over green stalks and mut-
tering to myself about how they're doing. Shovel and seeds in
hand, I became a gardener.

The thing about having a flower garden is that it's not as straightforward as you might think. Yes, you can just put seeds in the ground, water them, and wait. But after my first year, I learned that there were other important practices required to make blooms abundant. There's deadheading—making sure you pluck any wilting or rotting blooms right away before the plant spends energy producing seeds. There's the need to fertilize at the right times, thinning seedlings in a way that allows them to grow large, and weeding regularly as you keep an eye out for pests. And early on, when the seeds are sprouting and the garden is getting established, there's the need for pinching.

Pinching is the practice of cutting back a new and fast-growing plant to a lower set of leaves to force it to grow more stems or branches. Some gardeners literally reach down with their hands and "pinch" the stem between their fingers while others use a pair of sharp gardening shears to get just the right cut. This practice works for many types of flowers—zinnias, dahlias, cosmos, and snapdragons (just to name a few). Pinching can cause a single plant to produce double or triple the blooms, but it prolongs the blooming process by several weeks. The flowers come later, but they are more abundant.

The first time I pinched a plant, I was nervous. I saw my healthy, lovely flower garden springing up and thought it would look quite nice just as it was. It seemed cruel and counterintuitive to make a deep cut in the stem before it had even reached maturity. I even feared I would kill off my whole garden or prevent the plants from blooming altogether. But listening to skilled gardener wisdom, I grimaced, took my scissors, and started slicing back stems. Nothing happened right away. My previously full garden looked like it had been visited by a herd of deer. I worried that I'd backtracked. But a couple of weeks later, I noticed something—two or three stems grew healthy and strong where I'd made my cuts. Though I had delayed the big floral reveal, I could tell the garden would be bigger and better than ever. And I was amazed.

There's a lot of garden imagery in the Bible, and for good reason. God has written principles for life into all creation, and we see the way he works in the way plants are designed. The need for thinning, pinching, and pruning helps us understand why God reaches into our lives and makes a cut. As we feel weakened and frail and become familiar with loss, suffering, and waiting, we can grow discouraged. Initially, pruning and pinching seem to hurt a plant. But just as these techniques ultimately force more growth, God uses our struggles—seasons of sorrow and weakness, persecution or pain, deferred dreams and lost hopes—to encourage growth in us that leads to good fruit. Sometimes God makes us weak so we might become strong.

Jesus speaks of this process in the Gospel of John when he says we must be branches connected to him (John 15:1-17). Jesus is the vine and God the Father is the master gardener. While you might be tempted to think of a sweet old man shuffling gently around the vines, that is not the picture Jesus gives. Instead, the Vinedresser vigorously discards branches that don't produce fruit and prunes the ones that do, so they produce even more fruit. Charles Spurgeon, in preaching on this passage, said it this way:

> All the fruit-bearing saints must feel the knife. . . .
> But learn, beloved, especially you under trial, not
> to see an angry God in your pains or your losses,
> or your crosses; but instead thereof, see a hus-
> bandman, who thinks you a branch whom he
> estimates at so great a rate, that he will take the
> trouble to prune you, which he would not do if
> he had not a kind consideration towards you.[1]

What pains, losses, or crosses are in your life today? Have they left you feeling like a weakened stem or vine? Jesus says that this pruning produces fruit—the fruit of the Spirit. Though we may hope that someday our losses will amount to more accomplishments, a bigger following on social media, the family we've always dreamed of having, steady wisdom that others admire us for, or a retirement where we enjoy the sunshine and have a bunch of time to do nothing—this is not the fruit we're pruned for. In allowing us to have seasons of suffering and to feel our weakness and inability, the Lord means for us to look more like Christ, to have "love, joy, peace, patience, kindness, goodness, faithfulness, gentleness, self-control" in whatever circumstances or trials we face (Galatians 5:22-23). He means for us to cling with deeper dependence on and be fully fed by Christ alone.

As you consider the weakness of your current day or current season, ponder this: What if you're feeling the knife of the

---

1. Charles Spurgeon, "A Sharp Knife for the Vine Branches" (sermon, Metropolitan Tabernacle, October 6, 1867), Spurgeon Center, https://www.spurgeon.org/resource-library/sermons/a-sharp-knife-for-the-vine-branches/#flipbook/.

One who cultivates the land of your life—the husbandman? What if this pain is actually the sensation of pruning that leads to a stronger, healthier, more vibrant faith in Christ? What if this season will root you deeper into him and cause you to share the beauty and love of Christ with others? Jesus assures us that pruning is not primarily about pain but about joy (John 15:11). The pinching and the cutting back come from the hand of a loving God, committed to seeing you flourish and grow in true kingdom strength.

Additional Reading

> John 15:1-17
>
> Galatians 5:16-26
>
> 1 Peter 1:3-7

Questions for Reflection

I am weak

- In what areas of life do you feel the pruning shears? What things do you feel have been stripped away or lost, or have left you feeling weak or sorrowful?

- Can you think of a past season of life when God produced fruit in your life out of hardship or suffering? How does that give you hope in your season today?

He is strong

- What does John 15:1-17 tell you about God's heart and intention toward you in his pruning?

- What does true fruit or spiritual strength and health look like in God's garden? What aspects of this spiritual fruit will you pray for God to produce in your life through trials and weakness?

29

WHEN YOU'RE GOING TO BATTLE

*The word of God is living and active, sharper than
any two-edged sword, piercing to the division of
soul and of spirit, of joints and of marrow, and
discerning the thoughts and intentions of the heart.*

HEBREWS 4:12

When our oldest son was just sixteen months old, we brought his twin brothers home from the hospital. I knew raising three kids under two would be hard, but I had no idea what type of juggling it would require. Literally, I fed two infants on the couch while sliding a snack bowl to my whiny toddler with my foot. I pumped breast milk while I jostled two baby bouncers with my knees, using my teeth to grab a clean sock from my toddler's hand. My days were a rotation of picking people up and setting them back down—a game of tear-wiping whack-a-mole to comfort whoever was crying.

This was one of my weakest seasons of motherhood, when I hit my knees and begged God to divinely close all six eyes simultaneously so they'd all nap at once. *Please.* But when a year passed and they were all climbing onto countertops and dumping out spaghetti boxes before I could grab their chubby hands, I felt the weight of how my life and responsibilities had changed. Where before I managed stay-at-home-mom life by the seat of my pants—going for long walks and leisurely trips to the park—I now needed serious self-discipline, resolve, and structure to thrive. I needed God's help to grow my capacity and work ethic to match our family's age and stage.

In those years, the Lord drew me deep into his Word. He strengthened my hands with the book of Proverbs. Verses about diligence and hard work brought conviction in moments when I wanted to wallow in self-pity and overwhelm (Proverbs 13:4). He comforted me with good news from Paul's letter to the Romans. When I didn't accomplish all I'd hoped or I wrestled with mom guilt, God's Word reminded me that there was no condemnation for those who are in Christ Jesus (Romans 8:1). God gave me purpose in the mundane through scriptures that established every moment as a chance to worship and glorify him (Colossians 3:23). In my weakest moments, his living Word changed my life. This is what I hope you've experienced over the course of this devotional—seeing how God's Word has truth, help, and power in whatever weakness you're facing.

When I think of the power of God's Word in weakness, I

think of Jesus being tempted in the wilderness (Luke 4:1-12). For forty days, he went without food, community, or a soft place to lay his head. Surely in every human way he felt weak. When Satan tempted him to disobey God, Jesus didn't fight with physical violence, ignore him with breathing exercises, converse with crafty comebacks, or offer well-reasoned philosophical arguments. He went to battle with the sword of God's Word. For each temptation, Jesus recalled Scripture. He said, "It is written . . ." and he resisted.

Before we go too far, it's crucial to note that we are incapable of responding to temptation perfectly, even if we have God's Word at the ready. That's why Jesus is our Savior—because he is the only one who obeyed perfectly. But this account still shows that if God's Word is Christ's chosen defense, then it's strong enough for any battle we face.

In whatever weakness you're trudging through today, God's Word is living and active, able to pierce through the pain, doubt, or trial with hope. His Word tells the truth and sets us free (John 8:31-32; 14:6). It teaches us, corrects us, and equips us to do the things God has given us to do (2 Timothy 3:16-17). It's a light to our path, providing wisdom and guidance (Psalm 119:105). It works in our hearts to accomplish sanctification and God's plans for our lives (Isaiah 51:11; John 17:17; 1 Thessalonians 2:13). It helps us resist temptation and fight against sin (Psalm 119:11). It convicts us, humbles us, and causes us to worship the Lord (Hebrews 4:12).

Most of all, God's Word reminds us of whose story we're in and what role we play. It gives us the right perspective on our current trials as we consider our place in God's eternal plan.

Just as I talked in the first chapter about the panic of losing my phone and the tendency to not look in the obvious place first (hello, back pocket!), in our weakness, our first impulse is often to search for strength outside of God's Word. We try to fight with other weapons, and only when they fail us do we get desperate enough for the sword of Scripture.

In your next moment of weakness, consider going to battle with his Word in prayer *first*. Bring it to mind, sit and open your Bible, pull it up on your app, play it in your earbuds, sing it to yourself, write it on your hand, place it on a notecard above your sink—do whatever it takes to remember the strongest weapon of all.

⟫⟫ Additional Reading ⟪⟪

> Hebrews 4:1-16
> Luke 4:1-12
> 2 Timothy 3:16-17

⫸ *Questions for Reflection* ⫷

I am weak

- Describe a recent time in life when you felt like you wanted to "hit your knees" in weakness. What specific things did you need?

- In a weak moment, can you think of other defense mechanisms you've used that ultimately weren't effective or helpful?

He is strong

- In what ways does Jesus's perfect reliance on God's Word in his weakness and temptation give you confidence to rely on God's Word in your circumstances?

- How will you go to battle with God's Word today? (Hint: Try some of the examples in the last paragraph.)

30

WHEN YOU NEED SOMEONE STRONGER

*The mountains melt like wax before the L*ORD*, before the Lord of all the earth. The heavens proclaim his righteousness, and all peoples see his glory.*

PSALM 97:5-6

Most summers of my childhood included a road trip to Colorado. Before the era of tablets and smartphones, when even if you had access to the World Wide Web it was tethered to a cord in your house, we embarked on a twelve-hour drive across Kansas. It was just my brother and me in the back seat, armed with stickers, pencils, stuffed animals, home-made snacks, and the hope that we'd see enough cars in the middle of nowhere to spot states on license plates. More often than not, it was just endless wheatfields and relentless July sun for hours on end.

I loved crossing the Colorado border because I could start to look for the mountains. Eyes glued to the horizon, I'd squint for the first sign of the Rockies—slivers of dark gray almost indistinguishable from the atmosphere or large clouds. I'd often have one or two false alarms until the looming peaks were impossible to miss. The drive wasn't boring once I could see the mountains—they were all the entertainment I needed.

Now that I live in a notoriously flat state, the thought of seeing mountains puts a flutter in my stomach. I can close my eyes and visualize the streams between rock crevices, the flowers growing beside trails, and hear the snow crunching beneath my feet at a summit. The mountains are majestic. They make me feel small and weak. In most cases, I don't like feeling small and weak, but alongside the towering cliff faces I do—there in each grandiose shadow I am awe-inspired and certain that this world is wider than me and all the things I wrestle with and complain about. There, I get to see the beauty and complexity of creation and imagine what that says about the Creator himself. To rest in the assurance of a strength greater than my own.

The Bible says that mountains melt like wax before the Lord (Psalm 97:5). What does that even mean? How is that even possible? I could stand and kick a boulder at the base of a mountain all day and no one could ever tell I had put foot to rock. But the Lord has the strength to melt the whole thing like wax? *Wow*. I watch the lightning from my window, seeing how it splinters across the sky and rips off a tree branch. I have no say over where it goes and where it strikes. The Bible says that it is God who makes the lightning go wherever he pleases (Job 36:32, 37:3). What would it be like to have electrical charges spark on your command?

God's powerful reign doesn't stop there—it extends to the oceans, the sea creatures, the cattle on a thousand hills, and the rulers of nations. He reaches into the womb and into the grave—life and death are in his hands. He determines the times and places in which every person lives, and he knows every hair on every head. He can instantly heal any disease or disability and raise people from the dead. Look up into the night sky and think of the Creator who formed every gaseous star and created every planet. We think George Lucas is creative . . . all hail the great I AM.

If you believe God can do all that he pleases—in heaven and on earth, in the depths of the ocean, in the farthest corner of the universe, and in your own life—if you believe that his power and might and strength are ultimately used for good because he is good, then why is it so hard to rely on his strength? Sometimes I think it's hard because we're too busy to look at the horizon. We're too sucked into Twitter to marvel at the birds and see how he cares for them. We're too involved in our text chain to see the ways his endless creativity and beauty have colored the flowers. We're too obsessed with watching travel videos on TikTok to get out and hike a real trail.

In a world full of signs and screens, lights and laptops, concrete and steel, sometimes we need to stop and see the

Lord's strength around us, to think about all that he is, all that he owns, all that he can do. As we lift our eyes from our navel or our desk or our smartphone, we can find comfort in the Lord's sufficiency and gain new confidence as we bring all of our cares and concerns to him.

When I was a girl, my grandparents owned hundreds of acres of land in a remote part of central Missouri. I loved to visit there to see my family, of course, but there was something else that drew me, even before I truly understood and accepted the gospel. Twelve-year-old me would have fumbled to explain something about experiencing God on the land. Feeling close to him and knowing that he truly exists. Even before I knew what prayer really did or had the help of the Spirit, I would talk to God on the hillside. I would pray as I walked through the forest. I would pray as I lay under the stars. Creation compelled me to cry out to God.

Today, as you go about life and see your many weaknesses, make time to meditate deeply on God's strength—on the awesome "Lord of all" that he is. Maybe as you get smaller and smaller and he gets bigger and better, a new peace will come. You'll ask for his help and rest in confident faith that he'll give it. You'll pray for strength and know the storehouses are truly available. He owns them all.

⟫⟫ Additional Reading ⟪⟪

Psalm 97:1-7

Job 38:1–42:6

Psalm 8

⫸ Questions for Reflection ⫷

I am weak

- What do you spend most of your days looking at and focusing on? How does that impact your perspective on who you are in relation to God?

- In what areas of life do you most want to be in control or feel ownership over how things go?

He is strong

- Describe a time when you were in awe of God as you admired something in creation. Even if you can't go to that specific location again, what would it look like to step outside and admire his majesty in the creation around you today?

- In all the verses listed above, as you read about God's strength, power, and all that he created and controls, what truth stands out to you the most? How does this hearten you in your own weakness?

CONCLUSION: YES, JESUS LOVES ME

At some point or another, either right this moment, when you put the book down, later today, or weeks from now, you'll have an experience of feeling weak. Hopefully, as you worked through these thirty devotions, you noticed that not all weakness is the same. Weakness isn't categorically righteous or evil. It just depends on what you're talking about. So when your next instance of feeling weak settles in, instead of ignoring it, fighting it, or despairing in it, take a moment to simply notice it. Consider what that feeling is and where it's coming from and then ask the question "What type of weakness is this?"

WHAT TYPE OF WEAKNESS IS THIS?

Throughout the devotions, we saw that our weaknesses

generally fall into two different categories: weakness that results from God-given limitations, and weakness that's born from sin. As Paul says, weakness can be an incredible way for God's glory, power, and strength to be revealed in our lives (2 Corinthians 12:9). Jesus took on the weakness of human flesh and experienced things like physical hunger, grief, and persecution. If Jesus was "weak" in these ways, then we must caution ourselves against calling weakness "bad," despite the fact that our Western culture often does, and we must stop living with guilt and frustration about them. On the other hand, if we label all weakness as "godly," we might harden our hearts in an area where we need to repent. We might excuse an attitude or idol that is rooted in sin.

When we ask *What type of weakness am I experiencing?* we are determining which category our weakness comes from so we can address it correctly. Sometimes the answer to this question is not obvious or straightforward. A God-given limitation can be compounded with a heart that doesn't want to obey God. Similarly, a behavior that signals a sinful heart may be a misunderstanding of our personal limitations. As you decipher your own weaknesses, remember to ask God and the people who know and love you to help you consider each category with wisdom. As you do that, on the following pages are some ways to begin deciphering between the two.

I describe these indicators as examples because these lists could go on and on. Additionally, most things in life are far more complex than a list allows for, so I recognize there might be overlap here.

LIVING WITH GOD-GIVEN LIMITATIONS

These result from your humanity, the way God uniquely created you, or the circumstances he's given you:

- Reaching or recognizing the limits of your personal physical strength

- Needing sleep, food, water, shelter, safety, and so on—basic needs that cause real reactions and experiences of weakness if you don't have them

- Living with effects of disease, chronic illness or pain, paralysis, injury, and so on

- Grieving a significant loss or bereavement

- Undergoing persecution and trials in life or ministry

- Being naturally less competitive and driven (this one can dip into sinful weakness, but it's important to recognize that God didn't give every person the same temperament, internal drive, or capacity)

- Being a certain age or having a certain cognitive ability or maturity level

- Being under the authority of others and having less power

- Experiencing the normal weariness that comes from pouring out in ministry to others

SIGNS OF SINFUL BEHAVIOR

These are things we desire from the flesh that make it hard to walk in faith and obey God's commands:

- Living with patterns of laziness or sloth

- Being weighed down and ineffective because of unconfessed sin

- Lacking the fruit of self-control and discipline with things that matter for eternity

- Giving up or giving in easily, often at the first sign of temptation or struggle

- Lacking fortitude and refusing to believe God's promises in the midst of hard things

- Having a "weak conscience," being hypersensitive and strict about potentially crossing boundary lines, or disregarding all boundaries

- Lacking discernment skills: a roaming eye for truth, always learning but never arriving at the knowledge of the truth

- Acting in cowardice instead of bravery and boldness by putting on the armor of God

- Building the house of your life on sand instead of rock

Hopefully seeing these lists written out this way can get you thinking about what type of weakness you're dealing with and where these feelings came from.

WHAT'S NEXT?

Our evaluation helps us align our life with God's Word, instruction, comfort, encouragement, and love. Each category takes us down a slightly different path.

Knowing that life is rarely this clear-cut, if you think you are wrestling with feelings of weakness that result from your God-given limits:

- *Remember that Jesus loves you.* Consider how his love and sacrifice motivate your love for others in difficult circumstances (Ephesians 5:2).

- *Pray for contentment* in the circumstances God has given you, that you would receive all things with thanksgiving (1 Thessalonians 5:16-18). Your feelings of weakness might not go away, but perhaps he will help you understand and appreciate some of his purposes in them.

- *Look to Christ for joy* as you endure trials and feelings of weakness (Romans 12:12; James 1:2). Do this by reading about him and his promises in Scripture, thinking on those truths, praying, talking with other believers about him, and singing songs with rich truths.

- *Consider how God might be growing your endurance and character* as you walk through this weakness (Romans 5:3). Keep a journal and write down specific areas where you've asked God for help and how he's provided and changed your heart.

- *Seek wisdom and counsel from others* about how you might practically get through this season of weakness with the grace and help you need (Proverbs 19:8). Bring others alongside you for support, gather ideas for lifestyle or habit changes, and consider getting counseling if needed.

On the other hand, if after reflection and prayer with humility, you believe your feelings of weakness result from misalignment with God's commands and ways:

- *Remember that Jesus loves you.* While you were still a sinner, he died for you. He came with compassion for sinners, and he is near to the contrite (Psalm 51:17).

- *Pray and confess* your desires, struggles, and sins to God and receive mercy. Also consider talking about your issues with a trusted friend, spouse, pastor, or mentor who can point you to Christ and gently walk with you through them (Proverbs 28:13; James 5:16).

- *Seek wisdom and help* for how to practically go to battle against this temptation in your life. Put on the armor of God as you move forward (James 1:5; Ephesians 6:10-18). Research and gather ideas for lifestyle or habit changes, and consider getting counseling if needed.

- *Remember the Spirit lives in you* if you're a follower
  of Christ, giving you boldness, help, and strength
  to endure temptation and grow in Christlikeness.
  You are not without hope (Galatians 5:16)! Post
  this verse in your house and actively seek to pray
  and remember his help when you are tempted
  and struggling.

- *Spend time studying or memorizing passages of
  Scripture,* maybe even verses that specifically
  pertain to your struggle (Psalm 119:11). While
  topical word studies aren't always the best way to
  go through Scripture, they can be helpful when
  trying to understand what God's Word says on a
  given subject.

Though you might not see immediate results with any of
these practices, walk forward in faith that God can do more
than you can ever think or imagine (Ephesians 3:20).

YES, JESUS LOVES YOU

Perhaps you noticed a common thread between these two
categories. Regardless of what type of weakness you feel, Jesus
loves you. The Bible tells you so. In either weakness, Jesus is
strong.

The four Gospels share incredible accounts of Jesus's
life, death, and resurrection. They were not comprehensive
accounts (John 21:25), but they were an inspired compilation
of stories from his life—the ones God wanted to emphasize. So
whatever the Gospels contain, we can be sure that it's exactly

what God wanted us to know about his Son. Interestingly, in the midst of the incredible story of his coming, ministry, sacrifice, resurrection, and ascension, we see vignettes of the people Jesus spent his time with.

If a king were coming to a town, you would think he'd meet with the most important leaders. Sure, maybe he'd shake a few hands with the peasants and kiss a few babies, especially if he was unpopular or unknown and trying to win the goodwill of the people. But likely, he'd call on the people who matter most in his kingdom—his court, local nobility, statesmen, and soldiers. He'd convene with those who benefitted his reign.

But when King Jesus left his heavenly throne and came to earth, he didn't primarily interact with the strong, wealthy, powerful, religious, or righteous. He came to see and heal the weak. These are the stories the Gospels emphasize. This is what God wants us to see about what Jesus is like and who he loves.

Let's just look at the types of people Jesus interacts with in the Gospel of Matthew, for instance:

- his parents (from humble backgrounds, his mom pregnant while yet unwed, his dad a carpenter)

- Nazarenes (though a prophetic location, Nazareth was considered a place nothing good could come from, and was later used as a contemptuous label for Jesus's disciples)[1]

- fishermen

---

1. John 1:46. BibleStudyTools.com, s.v., "Nazarene," https://www.biblestudytools.com/dictionary/nazarene/.

- the prophet John the Baptist (though well known in his region, he still lived in the desert and had odd habits, unusual attire, and unpopular words of repentance and rebuke, which later led to his execution)

- the sick (usually this specifically meant they had a disease or illness)

- the afflicted (can mean physical pain or ailment, or any number of things that persistently bother someone, like a mental illness, grief, or persecution)

- those oppressed by demons

- epileptics

- paralytics

- lepers (those suffering from a skin disease that many at that time would have considered given by God as a judgment for sin, and that caused someone to be cut off from God's people, a symbol of separation from God)

- a gentile centurion (gentiles were outside of God's chosen people, viewed as sinful or unclean)

- hungry crowds

- women (Jesus heals and interacts with many women who, as a category, were considered weak and "less than" in that culture)

- children (as a category, they were considered weak, without value in that culture until they were older, a burden or dependent)
- tax collectors (viewed as greedy and dishonest)
- sinners
- blind men
- mutes
- the harassed and helpless (Jesus speaks of these people as sheep without a shepherd)
- a man with a crippled hand
- disciples (reminder, these were not the Jewish "in" crowd!)
- doubters
- "wise men" (came to visit him after his birth, one of the most positive depictions of strong and socially powerful people who worship Jesus)
- Jewish people (a people oppressed by foreign rulers)
- Pharisees (followed specific rules and traditions and believed in the resurrection)
- a rich young ruler
- elders
- priests (official office given by God in the Old Testament law)

- scribes (experts in the law, known for drafting legal documents)

- guards and soldiers

Though there are a few of the "elite" or socially well-off on this list, you can see that Jesus is recorded as spending a disproportionately large amount of time and ministry with those who were weak in some way.

Let that sink in for a moment. Think of yourself and the weaknesses you experience. Do you see yourself on that list? As I've processed through my own feelings of weakness, Jesus's presence comforts me and anchors me to the truth. I'm not left alone to decipher, defend, or soothe my weakness. Jesus's ministry to the weak extends to me even now. And Jesus has mercy and compassion on you too. Jesus is present with us in our weakness.

In the beatitudes, part of his famous Sermon on the Mount, Jesus shares a list of people who are blessed and cared for in some way: the poor in spirit, the mourners, the meek, the hungry, the merciful, the pure in heart, the peacemakers, the persecuted, and the reviled (Matthew 5:3-12). These qualities don't describe what we typically think of as the modern ideal. Jesus could have described any type of person or experience of life he wanted—he wasn't catering or pandering to the group in front of him. He spoke the truth: He is the way, the truth, and the life; he is the good shepherd and welcomes weak, hurting, needy sheep—those who know their need for him.

Because of this, we can let the chorus of the hymn "Jesus

Loves Me" wash over us again and again. Through frustration, through tears, in a whisper, or belted out loud. In hard days, weeks, or decades. We can sing,

> *Yes, Jesus loves me! Yes, Jesus loves me!*
> *Yes, Jesus loves me. The Bible tells me so.*

ACKNOWLEDGMENTS

Writing a devotional on weakness isn't done without the strength, support, and encouragement of others. To my husband, Brad, you were the first person to help me move this concept forward, and you pointed out the connection to the hymn "Jesus Loves Me." There is no way I could have done this without your unwavering support. To Laura Wifler, you were my biggest cheerleader and knew me well enough to tell me the tough stuff. You always asked how it was going, listened to my insecurities, and reminded me of the bigger picture. To Eric Schumacher, thank you for encouraging me to write a book on this topic. A huge thanks to Lauren Washer, Joanna Kimbrell, Eric Schumacher, Laura Wifler, Andrew Wolgemuth, and Brad Jensen for reading and offering feedback on early drafts of this devotional. I know it took a lot of time, but your feedback helped me hit my stride and made it a better devotion. Kelsey Hency, you are an incredible editor and helped me clarify my words, concepts, and theology with expert precision. To my literary agent, Andrew Wolgemuth, thank you for championing this project every step of the way. I'm grateful I can rely on your wisdom. To Kyle Hatfield and the whole team at Harvest House, you all are awesome. I couldn't imagine better publishing partners for this book. To my gospel life group at GABC, thank you for your faithful prayers as I wrote this book. Lewis, Gabe, Cal, Jones, and Evie, thank you for sacrificing, being flexible, and giving Mommy time to write this. I treasure all of you! (And see, your names made it into the book!) To my parents, Henry and Gayla, and my in-laws, Dean and Dianne, thank you for your cheerful and practical support during this process. Most importantly, I give thanks to you, Lord. You rescued me from my ultimate weakness and show your continued strength and love in my life. All of this is from you and to you and is given in service, however you may use it.

ABOUT EMILY

Emily A. Jensen is an author, podcaster, and the cofounder and content director at Risen Motherhood, where she and her sister-in-law, Laura Wifler, help moms connect their faith to their everyday lives. Emily's greatest passion is knowing Christ and making him known—in her home, her community, and to the ends of the Internet.

When she's not writing, speaking, podcasting, or encouraging women on Instagram, you can find her prepping a meal, pulling weeds, playing in the backyard with her children, or huddled up with a good book.

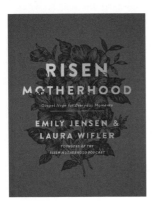

Speaking of good books, Emily is the coauthor of *Risen Motherhood* which has sold over 100,000 copies and been translated into multiple languages. Along with Laura, Emily walks readers through the redemptive story and reveals how the gospel applies to moms' everyday lives, bringing hope, freedom, and joy in every area of motherhood.

Emily lives in central Iowa with her husband and their five children.

Learn more about Emily and the *Risen Motherhood* book at **EmilyAJensen.com.**